933

£6·95

5839
(8)

D0346106

NEW ESSAYS ON
A FAREWELL TO ARMS

★ The American Novel ★

GENERAL EDITOR

Emory Elliott
University of California, Riverside

New Essays on
A Farewell to Arms

Edited by

Scott Donaldson

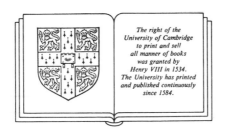

The right of the
University of Cambridge
to print and sell
all manner of books
was granted by
Henry VIII in 1534.
The University has printed
and published continuously
since 1584.

CAMBRIDGE UNIVERSITY PRESS

Cambridge

New York   Port Chester   Melbourne   Sydney

Published by the Press Syndicate of the University of Cambridge
The Pitt Building, Trumpington Street, Cambridge CB2 1RP
40 West 20th Street, New York, NY 10011, USA
10 Stamford Road, Oakleigh, Melbourne 3166, Australia

Cambridge University Press 1990

First published 1990

Printed in the United States of America

Library of Congress Cataloging-in-Publication Data

New essays on A Farewell to arms / edited by Scott Donaldson.
p. cm – (The American novel)
ISBN 0–521–38308–0. – ISBN 0–521–38732–9 (pbk.)
1. Hemingway, Ernest, 1899–1961. Farewell to arms. 2. World War,
1914–1918 – Literature and the war. I. Donaldson, Scott.
II. Series.
PS3515.E37F356   1990
813'.52–dc20   90–34341

British Library Cataloguing in Publication Data

New essays on A farewell to arms. – (The American novel).
1. Fiction in English. American writers. Hemingway,
Ernest, 1899–1961
I. Donaldson, Scott II. Series
813.52

ISBN 0–521–38308–0 hardback
ISBN 0–521–38732–9 paperback

Contents

Contents

Series Editor's Preface

In literary criticism the last twenty-five years have been particularly fruitful. Since the rise of the New Criticism in the 1950s, which focused attention of critics and readers upon the text itself – apart from history, biography, and society – there has emerged a wide variety of critical methods which have brought to literary works a rich diversity of perspectives: social, historical, political, psychological, economic, ideological, and philosophical. While attention to the text itself, as taught by the New Critics, remains at the core of contemporary interpretation, the widely shared assumption that works of art generate many different kinds of interpretation has opened up possibilities for new readings and new meanings.

Before this critical revolution, many American novels had come to be taken for granted by earlier generations of readers as having an established set of recognized interpretations. There was a sense among many students that the canon was established and that the larger thematic and interpretative issues had been decided. The task of the new reader was to examine the ways in which elements such as structure, style, and imagery contributed to each novel's acknowledged purpose. But recent criticism has brought these old assumptions into question and has thereby generated a wide variety of original, and often quite surprising, interpretations of the classics, as well as of rediscovered novels such as Kate Chopin's *The Awakening*, which has only recently entered the canon of works that scholars and critics study and that teachers assign their students.

The aim of The American Novel Series is to provide students of American literature and culture with introductory critical guides to

American novels now widely read and studied. Each volume is devoted to a single novel and begins with an introduction by the volume editor, a distinguished authority on the text. The introduction presents details of the novel's composition, publication history, and contemporary reception, as well as a survey of the major critical trends and readings from first publication to the present. This overview is followed by four or five original essays, specifically commissioned from senior scholars of established reputation and from outstanding younger critics. Each essay presents a distinct point of view, and together they constitute a forum of interpretative methods and of the best contemporary ideas on each text.

It is our hope that these volumes will convey the vitality of current critical work in American literature, generate new insights and excitement for students of the American novel, and inspire new respect for and new perspectives upon these major literary texts.

Emory Elliott
University of California, Riverside

1

Introduction

SCOTT DONALDSON

A *Farewell to Arms* made Hemingway a famous author. Published just as he passed his thirtieth birthday, it brought him the kind of public and critical acclaim he had been seeking since he had decided, in the aftermath of his wounding in 1918, to become a writer. During the ten-year interim, he had worked effectively as a foreign correspondent and then abandoned that career to devote all his energy to fashioning the understated and pared-away prose style that was his most important legacy to twentieth-century literature. At first it was difficult to place this new kind of writing. His stories were interesting, editors acknowledged, but they read like sketches or *contes*, not ordinary fiction. The breakthrough occurred at mid-decade, when the stories and novels came with a rush. Between 1923 and 1927 Hemingway published two slim volumes from small presses in Paris and four hardcover books in the United States. The best known of these was *The Sun Also Rises* (1926), a novel that caused something of a sensation. On the surface, *Sun* appeared to celebrate an expatriate world of drinking and sex. He had written "one of the filthiest books of the year," his mother wrote him, and many agreed with her. This, of course, was a drastic misreading of a novel that Hemingway insisted was a "very moral book." He did not mind confounding the expectations of genteel readers, but he did want to be taken seriously. His next novel, he realized, should address a major theme, and two of the great themes were love and war.

Though in 1924 he started and soon gave up on an autobiographical novel about his war experiences, tentatively entitled "Along with Youth," the war was very much in the background of many of his best stories. Late in 1926 and early in 1927 he wrote

1

two stories closely based on his traumatic wounding in July 1918. "Now I Lay Me" described the sleeplessness he suffered after being blown up at night on the Austrian front. "In Another Country," with its opening sentence that F. Scott Fitzgerald so admired – "In the fall the war was always there, but we did not go to it any more" – recalled the therapy he had undergone for his leg at Milan's Ospedale Maggiore. Both stories raised the possibility that marriage might somehow relieve the anguish of the wounded soldier, and both rejected that possibility. He was not yet ready to integrate the themes of love and war, and in a short story there wasn't enough space to accomplish such a complicated task.

The potentialities of such a novel must have been spinning around in his head – as Paul Smith demonstrates in his essay "The Trying-out of *A Farewell to Arms* – but it was not until March 1928 that he started a story that kept growing and eventually became *Farewell.* The novel was written and revised and proofed during the next fifteen months, in many different parts of the United States and Europe. Hemingway started it in Paris in March, continued at Key West, Florida, in April and early May, kept making progress during a visit to his wife Pauline's parents in Piggott, Arkansas, and during her delivery of their son Patrick in Kansas City, Missouri, in the heat of June and July, and completed his manuscript late in August after producing as many as seventeen pages a day in three separate locations around Sheridan, Wyoming. He was back in Key West to work on revisions in November, and his editor Max Perkins came down to collect the script and spend a week fishing late in January. Shortly thereafter Perkins wired an offer of $16,000 to serialize the novel in *Scribner's Magazine,* and Hemingway read proofs on the six-part serial version both in Key West and in France. He was still struggling with the ending of the book, however, and did not complete the final version until June 24, 1929, in Paris. The following month he was correcting book galleys in Spain, and finally, on September 27, Scribners brought out *A Farewell to Arms* at $2.50. It was an immediate success.[1]

Geography really didn't matter to a writer practicing his craft, Hemingway believed, and the composition of *Farewell* certainly illustrated the point. He wrote it in a series of strange rooms, living

2

out of suitcases. And he wrote it despite a series of daunting personal and professional complications. All that traveling about in 1928–9 reflected the still-unsettled state of his marriage to Pauline Pfeiffer, the woman for whom he had divorced his first wife, Hadley Richardson. Married in May 1927, he and the new Mrs. Hemingway decided to sink roots in the United States, especially because they were soon to become parents. Before they settled on Key West as the family home, however, the newlyweds were in a state of almost frantic movement. And Pauline's delivery, late in June, could hardly have been more difficult. Her life was manifestly in danger as she suffered through eighteen hours of labor and a cesarean section to give birth to their son. That crisis, resolved more painfully, Hemingway wrote into the final pages of *A Farewell to Arms*.

Early December produced another family misfortune, this time fatal. Depressed, in poor health, and worried about his financial affairs, Ernest's father shot himself in his bedroom at Oak Park, Illinois. "I was very fond of him and feel like hell about it," Hemingway wrote Max Perkins. But as eldest son, he also felt an obligation to see to the welfare of his mother and the two children still at home. Dr. C. E. Hemingway had left "damned little money" for their support, and the thing for Ernest to do, he wrote Perkins, was to keep on with *Farewell* so that he could help them out.[2]

The professional difficulties that lay ahead were primarily concerned with the book's acceptability. In at least five different ways, *Farewell* violated conventional standards and aroused the objection of one group or another. It used the vulgar language of the troops. It depicted an illicit love affair in basically sympathetic terms. It described Catherine's deathbed anguish in excruciating detail. It did not sufficiently condemn Frederic's desertion from the Italian army. It presented a disturbingly vivid account of the Italian army's collapse in 1917.

Max Perkins was particularly concerned about the language of the novel, just as he had been in the case of *Sun*. In re-creating the background of men at war, Hemingway reproduced some of their barracks talk. Not to do so, he felt, would present a false view of an essentially brutal life. Soldiers at the front swore as naturally and consistently as they patronized whorehouses, and so it should be in *Farewell*. Perkins, however, worried about the probable outrage of readers unaccustomed to seeing such words in print. This was especially true in regard to the serialization of the book in *Scribner's Magazine*. The magazine had a family readership, he explained to Ernest, and certain words and even passages would have to be omitted in the serial. Happy with his $16,000 magazine sale, the largest yet paid by *Scribner's*, Hemingway consented. Words and phrases could be cut, but blank spaces or ellipses should be inserted to indicate the cuts. Emasculation was "a small operation," but not one to be undertaken lightly.

When Robert Bridges, editor of the magazine, sent Hemingway the proofs of the first installment on February 19, he called attention to the use of dashes in place of words that might be thought inappropriate in the high school classrooms that used *Scribner's* for supplementary reading. It would be different with the book, he said. They were using the novel to lead off their May issue and planned to run it in six installments. At that stage, Hemingway began to worry about the Italian response, and he composed a disclaimer to accompany the June issue. Although *Farewell* was written in the first person, he pointed out, it was "not autobiographical" and was "no more intended as a criticism of Italy or Italians" than Shakespeare's *Two Gentlemen of Verona*. When the proofs of the second installment reached him, he discovered that Bridges had made two substantial cuts – one of six lines in the manuscript, the other of ten lines – without consulting him. That was not something he had agreed to, and he exploded in an angry letter to Perkins that he would rather return the money than permit arbitrary eliminations. Half of his writing consisted in elimination, and if someone else was also going to be cutting, then let that person sign the book too. That was on March 11, and eleven days later, after assurance from Perkins that he anticipated no further changes (other than blanks for coarse language), Hemingway calmed down. Let the cuts stand, he wrote his editor.[3]

When the book galleys arrived in June, however, Hemingway once more reacted with indignation. The very words that Perkins wanted to delete – "balls," "shit," "fuck," "cocksucker," for example – he could find in Erich Maria Remarque's *All Quiet on the Western Front*, the war novel that had become a best-seller in Germany and England and was about to be published in the United States. For him to leave out the way soldiers actually talked would weaken *Farewell*. But, he added, if using the words meant that the book would be suppressed, he would go along with the omissions.[4] Before the month was out, suppression emerged as a very real possibility.

On June 20, Michael H. Crowley, Boston's police chief, barred the June issue of *Scribner's Magazine* from the bookstands of the city because part of the installment of *Farewell* was deemed salacious. What bothered the Boston censors, and what bothered most of the readers who canceled their subscriptions to the magazine, was not the language of the book so much as the subject matter, particularly the love affair between the unmarried protagonists. "What modernists call realism," an outraged gentleman from Maine wrote, "reminds me of an artist picking out for a still life picture a half empty milk bottle with milk souring and the flies crawling over it, some stale and rotting vegetables, and moldy bread." Some kitchens looked like that, he realized, but they did not interest him as "a permanent exhibit" on his wall.[5] Such a reaction seems quaint sixty years later, and being banned in Boston has become something of a joke in the interim, but Scribners took the news very seriously at the time.

In a carefully worded statement, the publishers called the Boston police chief's action "an improper use of censorship." It was wrong to base objections on certain passages without taking into consideration "the effect and purpose of the story as a whole." In its overall effect, *Farewell* was "distinctly moral. It is the story of a fine and faithful love, born, it is true, of physical desire." If good can come from evil, then the writer must be allowed to describe the conditions from which the good evolves. If white is to be contrasted with black, then a picture cannot be all white. But, the statement concluded, Hemingway's novel was neither a moral tract nor — as some seemed to think it — an example of antiwar propaganda. It was a story by "one of the finest and most highly regarded of the modern writers," and it would continue to run in *Scribner's Magazine* for the next four issues. Sales of all those issues were forbidden in Boston.[6]

Book banning in Boston was already an old story in 1929, but prohibiting the sale of a magazine in which a book was appearing was a new development, and the censorship engendered nation-wide publicity. That was not all bad, of course. "Many readers had doubtless missed Mr. Hemingway's powerful story," the *New York Herald Tribune* commented, "and they will be grateful to the [Boston police] chief for calling their attention to it." The magazine sales were not much affected, with increased circulation outside Massachusetts making up for what was lost there. The book itself stood to profit from the notoriety, but Perkins took little pleasure in that circumstance. "I hate the publicity, greatly helpful as it may turn out to be," he wrote Hemingway on June 27. It cast a "deeply significant and beautiful" book in an unhealthful and prejudicial light. And it increased the likelihood that the book might be suppressed. There were three words (Perkins could not bring himself to set them down on paper) that might prompt legal action. One of these was so objectionable that it "might turn a judge right around against us, and to the post office, it and the others, I think, would warrant (technically) action." Besides, he pointed out, it would be a dirty shame to have Hemingway associated with the purveyors of smut. On July 12, Perkins reiterated his fears. They had decided against taking the Boston ban to court, because that seemed unlikely to accomplish anything of importance. Besides, "there is still . . . considerable anxiety for fear of the federal authorities being stirred up. They seem to take curious activity of late, and if the post office should object, we would be in Dutch."[7]

With the threat of legal and governmental suppression so firmly established, Hemingway acceded to Perkins's deletion of gutter language (most of it uttered during the chaos of the retreat from Caporetto). "I understand . . . about the words you cannot print – if you cannot print them – and I never expected you could print the one word (C-S) that you cannot and that lets me out." Yet where such sanctions were not involved, he stuck to his guns. On August 16, Perkins sent *Farewell*'s English publisher, Jonathan Cape, two sets of galleys, one with the offending words blanked out, the other with the words spelled out "if you feel they can be, and according to the author's wish."[8]

Perkins also moved to protect Hemingway's reputation through the assistance of Owen Wister, author of *The Virginian*, friend and biographer of Theodore Roosevelt, and highly respected literary elder statesman. Wister had come to Hemingway's defense when *Sun* had been under attack, and now he did so again, despite certain reservations about *Farewell*. Wister read the new novel well in advance of publication and wrote Perkins on April 30 that he thought the book "many jumps of seven league boots ahead of anything he has done so far." But he found it "too outspoken in its medical details. . . . They are so terrible and so powerful that I personally shrank from them as I read." It would be better, he thought, if Hemingway could leave out the ether and communicate Catherine's agony by suggestion. "They've got to give me something," she might say, and that would be enough to make the point. But Wister was not adamant on this subject, and when he and Hemingway dined together in Paris in the wake of the Boston ban, they got along famously. Some weeks later Wister did write to Hemingway with his suggestions for revision, which Hemingway acknowledged without adopting. "Your advice is always good and I will take all I can of it," he replied. He didn't take much, and he was decidedly annoyed when, even after publication, Wister marked up a copy of the book and sent it to Hemingway as instruction on "what to put in as important and what to leave out as immaterial."

Immediately after the Boston ban, however, Wister rallied to Hemingway's cause with a public expression of praise. *Farewell* was far better than his earlier work, Wister asserted. "He had got rid of those jolty Western Union ten word sentences . . . and also of that monotony which came of dealing too much in human garbage. This book is full of beauty and variety, and nobody in it is garbage." In addition, he endeavored to make an asset of the book's frankness by comparing it to the work of Defoe. Hemingway, like Defoe, was "lucky to be writing in an age that will not stop its ears at the unmuted resonance of a masculine voice."[9]

As Perkins had anticipated, the publicity about *Farewell* generated a good deal of interest, and Scribners ran off a first printing of 31,050 copies for the September 27 publication of the book. (By way of contrast, the firm had issued *Sun* in a first printing of 6,000, with two additional printings of 2,000 each within the first few months. Eventually, of course, both novels sold millions of copies.) "FIRST REVIEW SPLENDID STOP PROSPECTS BRIGHT," Perkins wired Hemingway on September 28, and then "ALREADY GETTING REORDERS STOP VERY FINE PRESS" on October 3. By that time, they had ordered a second printing of 10,000 copies, and several other printings followed during the fall. Early in January, sales passed 70,000 copies, and *Farewell* occupied a strong position on the bestseller lists in competition with, among others, Remarque's *All Quiet.*[10]

Save for a few adamant defenders of literary respectability, *Farewell* took the reviewers by storm. Without understanding the novel in any deep or lasting sense, they nonetheless recognized that it was a remarkable performance. "I have finished *A Farewell to Arms* and am still a little breathless, as people are after a major event in their lives," James Aswell commented in the *Richmond Times-Dispatch*. John Dos Passos, writing in *The New Masses*, called the book "a first-rate piece of craftsmanship by a man who knows his job," and lest that sound like faint praise, he went on to mention half a dozen brilliant passages that "match up as narrative prose with anything that's been written since there was any English language." Clifton Fadiman touted the novel for the Pulitzer Prize (it did not win). In England, J. B. Priestley suggested that before long readers might be able to boast of owning a first edition of *A Farewell to Arms*, and Arnold Bennett called it "strange and original," yet "superb."[11]

Several reviewers detected the influence of Sherwood Anderson and, especially, Gertrude Stein in Hemingway's prose. In its reliance on simple speech and repetition, *Farewell* seemed to be following the lead of Stein's *Three Lives*, with the difference – as Fanny Butcher pointed out in the *Chicago Tribune* – that in the case of Hemingway one could be "perfectly clear" about what he was saying. "Ernest Hemingway," she wrote, "is the direct blossoming of Gertrude Stein's art." Then there was the question of Hemingway's influence on others. As Malcolm Cowley observed, "he is imitated by writers much older than himself – a rare phenomenon

– and one finds traces of his influence almost everywhere." This was particularly noticeable in connection with what Cowley called Hemingway's "subtractive" method. From the novel of previous generations, "he has subtracted the embellishments; he has subtracted all the descriptions, the meditations, the statements of theory and he has reserved only the characters and their behavior – their acts, their sensual perceptions, their words." Henry Hazlitt agreed, but found the influence lamentable. Already one could see signs of a Hemingway school springing up, and the young writers who seemed to idolize him might well find better models to imitate. The "hard, clean, athletic" quality of Hemingway's prose tended to become dull after a time, Hazlitt felt, and was ill-suited for conveying "nuances, shades and subtleties."[12]

Yet that very subtractive style, as Cowley was the first to recognize, bespoke the man and what he had to say about his times. If he was already "mentioned with the respect that one accords to a legendary figure," it was because he "expressed, better than any other writer, the limited viewpoint of his contemporaries, of the generation which was formed by the war and which [was] still incompletely demobilized." "In this book," as Henry Seidel Canby put it, "you get your own times . . . to wonder about and interpret."[13] This does not, of course, mean that *Farewell* is significant only as a portrait of the generation that went to war and later became bitterly disillusioned. The novel has deeper resonances than that and continues to speak to succeeding generations, but it also evokes the climate of opinion of a particular period. One can say as much of only a few works in the canon of American literature, such as *Huckleberry Finn*, for instance, or *The Waste Land*.

Generally, the early reviews found *Farewell* to be an advance beyond *Sun*. Both books portrayed a world in the throes of despair, but the hopelessness of *Sun* gave way to a kind of affirmation in its successor. As Bernard De Voto put it, the "new book has what its predecessor lacked, passion. It has, too, a kind of sublimity." The subject matter itself contributed to that effect. Fishing, drinking, and bullfighting might not be the stuff of tragedy, but love and death assuredly were. Arnold Bennett had his reservations on this score, however. He thought Hemingway "undecided whether he [was] writing a description of the war as his hero saw it, or the love-story of his hero." Oddly, that was precisely what Perkins considered the book's "one serious flaw" — that its two great themes of love and war were not sufficiently tied together.[14]

For the most part, the early commentators thought the love affair itself honestly rendered, idyllic, moving, "charged with sentiment, beauty, and tragedy," comparable to the story of Romeo and Juliet or of Tristan and Iseult in its poignancy.[15] Yet to some, Frederic and Catherine seemed not fully realized characters, less real than the minor characters, basically uncomplicated, "a pair of silhouettes" with no discernible difference between them.[16] It would be a long while before critics came to recognize the complexity of the novel and its characterization.

From the beginning, though, two sections of the book were singled out for applause. The description of the Italian retreat from Caporetto was, Cowley observed, "perhaps the finest single passage that Hemingway has written." Canby called it "a masterly piece of reporting," evidently under the impression that the author was writing out of personal experience. The mistake was understandable; *Farewell* reads with great authenticity. But Hemingway was still worried about the book's reception in Italy (for good reason, because it was indeed banned in that country) and repeatedly asked Scribners to issue disclaimers to the effect that his story was fiction and was not based on actual characters or military units. Such a disclaimer did run in the front matter to the second printing, but then it disappeared, despite Hemingway's letter of November 30 to Perkins: "You will repeat again that it is fiction, that I lay no claim even to have been in Italy, that I would never attempt to judge or picture Italy or Italians as such, but that I have only taken advantage of the tradition by which writers from the earliest times have laid the scenes of their books in that country."[17]

The other passage that reviewers selected for commendation was the novel's ending. They found the final paragraph particularly effective, because its muted tone so well suited the emotional loss that Frederic had suffered.

> But after I had got them out and shut the door and turned out the light it wasn't any good. It was like saying good-by to a statue. After

10

a while I went out and left the hospital and walked back to the hotel in the rain.

You might think Hemingway's "absolutely brutal, cold blooded narrative" ill-suited for emotional effects, Butcher observed, but two different women she knew "were seized with . . . uncontrollable sobs" upon reading this conclusion.[18] To the extent that Hemingway was aware of this praise, he must have been pleased. He sweated over that ending as much as over anything he ever wrote.

Several early commentators addressed the issue of censorship, and almost all of them were in agreement that whatever had happened in regard to the magazine serial, the book should not be suppressed. Harry Hansen of the *New York World*, who had in June entitled a column on the Boston ban "Naughty Ernest," repeated his opinion that some passages could be accounted for only by attributing to the author "a mischievous desire to shock the eminently respectable." Ten years earlier, such a story "could not have been written, much less printed." But times had changed, and now "Hemingway can no more be banned than he can be ignored." *A Farewell to Arms* was "a red rag to the Boston bull," but in book form it was not censored even there.[19] It may be that police chief Crowley and the leaders of the city's Watch and Ward Society were mollified by the death of Catherine, an event that a narrow-minded reader could choose to interpret as a judgment against fornication.

Yet amid the general chorus of acclaim, a few dissonant voices could be heard bemoaning the novel's explicit language and unconventional love affair. Among the most strident was the writer for the *Newark News* who, in a review that appeared the day after publication, inveighed against "the preoccupation with sex from which Mr. Hemingway cannot, or perhaps will not, free himself." The trouble was that Hemingway was far from alone in that respect; in fact, he and "the other flingers of filth were constantly trying to outdo one another." If the trend were not reversed, current literature might soon sink "into a neurasthenic and phosphorescent decay." Nonetheless, the *News* acknowledged, *Farewell* amounted to an improvement on *Sun*, whose characters

11

"were for the most part degenerates." In *Farewell* they were "somewhat closer to normal, in that they are merely frankly sensual."[20]

Looking back over sixty years of literary history, it is difficult to understand the outrage expressed by a few of these first readers. "The obvious purpose of the story," one of them declared, was "to offer a vicarious satisfaction to those who are either too jaded or too timid to get the satisfaction in a normal way through natural experiences." The book should be classified as "venereal fiction." To another, Lieutenant Henry seemed an "utterly immoral" man who "took the woman of his desire as lightly as he deserted from his command in the Italian army." The issue of desertion troubled a number of reviewers, as did the novel's "biological and pathological data." Altogether, Hemingway was far too concerned with realistic detail, and not nearly enough with those "higher purposes" and "larger relations" that, these commentators agreed, constituted the proper province of fiction.[21]

By far the most troublesome of these attacks came from the well-known Chicago novelist and critic Robert Herrick, in a November 1929 article in *Bookman* entitled "What Is Dirt?" On the basis of his reading of the first two installments of *Farewell* in *Scribner's Magazine*, he was confident that Hemingway's novel could only be regarded as "dirt" or, in his misappropriation of Owen Wister's word, as "garbage." Herrick concentrated on two scenes that, he felt, demonstrated his contention. The first of these occurs on the train from the field hospital to Milan, when Frederic and another traveler get drunk on grappa and throw up. Such things certainly happened, Herrick admitted, but that did not give the creative artists license to depict them. Such a creator had a fundamental duty to "endow the activities he chooses to present" with significance, and in his judgment Hemingway had not done so. Therefore the scene was "just unpleasant garbage."

The other offending scene was the reunion of Frederic and Catherine in the Milan hospital, when he persuades her to make love. "This, I maintain, is merely another lustful indulgence, like so many that occur between men and women and have since the beginning of time and will persist to its end. It has no significance, no more than what goes on in a brothel, hardly more than the copulation of animals." Hemingway had converted what the blurb writers for the magazine called "beautiful love" into mere dirt.

Herrick concluded by comparing *Farewell* unfavorably with Remarque's *All Quiet*. Remarque's American publishers had deleted certain passages and altered others to soften coarse language, but in Herrick's judgment that had been a mistake. Americans needed to learn more about the realities of war and "should have received this important story unblemished by prudery, in its full import." On the other hand, to his way of thinking, "no great loss to anybody would result if *A Farewell to Arms* had been suppressed."[22]

This was too important an assault in too respected a journal to go unanswered, Perkins decided. But he discouraged Hemingway from responding himself. The best thing for the author to do, he advised Ernest, was "to treat such articles as Herrick's 'with the silent contempt they deserve'." Nor did he respond to the offer of young Thornton Wilder, who had won the Pulitzer Prize for his 1927 novel *The Bridge of San Luis Rey*, to align himself in defense of *Farewell* "with other and more authoritative enthusiasts." Instead, he complained directly to the editor of the magazine, and wrote Wister for his help yet again. Clearly, he pointed out, Herrick "misrepresents the book, and it seems to me most extraordinary that a man of [his] standing, all his life a writer and a teacher of literature, should give his judgment upon a book after having read not more than half of it." What was more, Herrick had willfully misrepresented Wister's views by summoning up his term "garbage" to convict the author. What Wister had emphasized, after all, was that no one in *Farewell* could rightly be classified as human garbage. This time, however, Wister declined the role of paladin. There was no need to worry about Herrick, he told Perkins; Herrick was a good deal of a prig and lacked a sense of humor – otherwise he would be a better novelist. Besides, "all this stuff really helps the book to be known. Once known, it will either sink or swim. My hope and conviction is that it will swim."[23]

In the end the reply to Herrick came from two unanticipated sources, neither of whom supported the novel as vigorously as it deserved. Three months after "What Is Dirt?" appeared, *Bookman* ran a long discussion of the article by Henry Seidel Canby. Canby corrected Herrick for misappropriating Wister's comment, and judged him unfair in jumping to conclusions about the novel without finishing it. Furthermore, he considered *Farewell* superior to *All Quiet:* "It is difficult to imagine ever finding interest in another book by Remarque; it is difficult to imagine finding any book by Hemingway not interesting." Otherwise, what Canby had to say was critical; he believed that Hemingway had "not had sufficient adverse criticism," and set out to repair the deficiency.

Specifically, Canby found fault with the depiction of the love affair and with the author's style. Herrick was right to call Frederic and Catherine's lovemaking "merely another lustful indulgence," because the basic story of the book was "of a Scotch nurse made irresponsible by heartbreak and an American soldier apparently irresponsible by nature going on an irresponsible honeymoon and getting away with it." As for Hemingway's style, Canby declared that it "has steadily deteriorated until it is now the worst of any widely acclaimed writer." He affected an illiteracy borrowed from Gertrude Stein, and aside from his "always masterly" dialogue, the narrative parts of the book were made "nearly unreadable" by the "droning beat of endless bald declarations, the maddening succession of 'and'-sentences, the unvarying monotone, the piling on of needless details, the eccentric punctuation." After such criticism, Canby concluded with the hope that Hemingway might transcend himself. His "career has only begun, and begun so strikingly that almost anything may be expected."[24]

The following month, in the March 1930 *Bookman,* Scribners finally managed to present its defense of Hemingway through the agency of M. K. Hare, of Tryon, North Carolina. After reading Herrick's article, Hare wrote an unsolicited letter to Scribners. Perkins liked it so much that he sent it on to *Bookman* as a letter to the editor. When the magazine refused it on that basis, Scribners paid to run it in the advertising columns. In this reply, Hare dealt forthrightly with Herrick's primary objections. The drunkenness and vomiting Herrick deplored in the novel were not instances of mere self-indulgence, he maintained, but could be traced directly to the stress of war. More importantly, Hare defended Hemingway's depiction of the love story on the grounds that sexual relations should no longer be treated "as a guilty secret." Besides, Hemingway had presented one of "the least affected and . . . most affecting pictures of what man and woman can mean to one another." *Farewell* might not be art, Hare conceded in a less than ringing conclusion, "but need it be called 'dirt'?"[25]

If the newspaper and magazine responses to *Farewell* prove anything, it is that early reviews of major books rarely achieve a high level of understanding. Despite occasional gleams of insight, nothing that was written in the months after publication approached a proper evaluation of the novel. An intelligent and perceptive criticism takes time to develop, a fact that makes Ford Madox Ford's introduction to the 1932 Modern Library edition all the more remarkable for its acuity.

Better than anyone else ever has, Ford described what it was that qualified Hemingway as an "impeccable writer of English prose," Canby to the contrary notwithstanding. Above all, he made the language seem new and alive. "[His] words strike you, each one, as if they were pebbles fetched fresh from a brook. They live and shine, each in its place." And what this novel demonstrated beyond doubt was that "Hemingway, the writer of short, perfect episodes, [could] keep up the pace through a volume." Unlike others thought of as stylists – Walter Pater, for example – his writing had no purple patches, no verbal felicities. "While you are reading [*Farewell*] you forget to applaud its author. You do not know that you are having to do with an author. You are living." It was this quality that made the book equally thrilling to people who had never read a book before and to those "who had read and measured all the good books in the world."[26]

Another introduction, Robert Penn Warren's to the 1949 edition of *Farewell*, brought the themes of the novel into focus for the first time. The book was an immediate success, Warren realized, because it "told a truth" about those who fought World War I and found their lives "wrenched from the expected pattern and the old values." These people had lost their bearings and felt themselves bereft, homeless, adrift. Yet in an apparently God-abandoned world, they were seeking a code by which to live. The love of Frederic and Catherine, begun on the level of appetite, develops into what Count Greffi calls "a religious feeling." In this sense, though concerned with secular and not divine love, *Farewell* should be regarded as a religious book.[27]

Carlos Baker's *Hemingway: The Writer as Artist* (1952) concentrated on the lovers' attempt to make a home for themselves in a chaotic war-tossed environment. Eager to establish Hemingway's artistry, Baker argued that the novel was constructed around the twin poles of Home and Not-Home, with the cool crisp mountains symbolizing the good place, and the hot and sweaty plains the opposite. In most respects, this symbolic pattern does indeed exist in *Farewell*. Frederic and Catherine experience their idyll in the mountains above Montreux, while at his most depraved he drinks and whores his way through a furlough in a series of low-lying Italian cities. But Hemingway refused to do violence to verisimilitude in constructing a symbolic framework for his novel, as E. M. Halliday pointed out in a 1956 essay. Catherine dies in Lausanne, for example, and Lausanne, standing on a series of steep hills, is "an extraordinarily poor specimen of a City of the Plain."[28]

Not even the rain, the most frequently discussed symbolic device in *Farewell*, functions with absolute consistency throughout the novel. It is true that Catherine sees herself dead in the rain, and it is in fact raining when she dies and Frederic walks back to his hotel alone. The rain brings the cholera, leads to Frederic's loss of his ambulance and his men during the retreat, and destroys the winter sport at the Guttingens'. Yet the lovers make their escape from Italy to Switzerland during a rainstorm on Lake Maggiore, and the storm helps them avoid getting caught. As Hemingway recognized, you can't write your symbols first; they have to develop out of the story, and not be applied to it artificially. Moreover, he was reluctant to tie his fiction up in neat packages for critical unwrapping.

Philip Young's *Ernest Hemingway: A Reconsideration*, also 1952, articulated his theory that Hemingway's work could best be understood in relation to the wounds he suffered in his youth, and in particular his traumatic wounding at Fossalta in July 1918. That theory has obvious relevance to *Farewell*, though, as we shall see, Hemingway took measures to distinguish his experience in the war from that of his protagonist. But Young's section on the novel was also noteworthy for pointing out how the themes of love and war are subtly paralleled. In regard to the war, Frederic Henry

16

"goes from desultory participation to serious action and a wound, and then through his recuperation in Milan to a retreat which leads to his desertion." His relationship with Catherine Barkley goes through "six precisely corresponding stages – from a trifling sexual affair to actual love and her conception, and then through her confinement in the Alps to a trip to the hospital which leads to her death."[29]

Walker Gibson's *Tough, Sweet & Stuffy: An Essay on Modern American Prose Styles* (1966) remains the most interesting of several attempts to illustrate how Hemingway's unusual prose style works in the context of the novel. With the aid of a "Style Machine" that measures the structure and length of sentences, the use of adjectives and adverbs, the proportion of verbs in the passive voice, and so on through sixteen criteria, Gibson was able to designate the narrative voice of Frederic Henry as that of a prototypical "Tough Talker." By that term Gibson meant someone who says what he means without apology or elaboration, someone who is suspicious of abstractions, someone who draws his reader into a kind of intimate communion by letting the reader make connections. As Gibson characterized him, "Frederic Henry is a hard man who has been around in a violent world, and who partially conceals his strong feelings behind a curt manner. . . . His tense intimacy with his assumed reader, another {wo}man who has been around, is implied by colloquial patterns from oral speech and by a high frequency of the definite article." In support of that last point, he cited *Farewell*'s opening sentence: "In the late summer of that year we lived in a house in a village that looked across the river and the plain to the mountains." What summer? What river, what plains, what mountains? Such questions we might well ask, for the definite articles attached to those nouns imply a knowledge we do not in fact share with the narrator who is speaking to us. But we do not ask those questions. The voice of Frederic Henry begins in the middle of the conversation; he talks to us as if we knew the answers to those questions, and we accept the implied intimacy.[30]

A significant breakthrough in the criticism of *Farewell* developed during the mid-1970s and was stimulated both by the opening of the Hemingway collection at the John F. Kennedy Library and by a surge of revisionist approaches to the novel. Michael S. Reynolds's

Hemingway's First War: The Making of "A Farewell to Arms" (1976) used his study of the Hemingway manuscripts to establish the importance of the author's revisions. His changes, Reynolds asserted, were as important as those of Keats, and indeed Hemingway's prose rewards – one might almost say *demands* – the same kind of close reading that illuminates poetry. But perhaps the principal contribution of Reynolds's book was to distinguish between Ernest Hemingway and his protagonist Frederic Henry. The teenager Hemingway was wounded on the Piave in the summer of 1918, after only a few weeks in Italy. Frederic Henry is much older; he has been studying architecture in Rome and knows his way around Italy. He lacks the innocent idealism about the war that led Hemingway to get involved. Yet his war lasts much longer – from the late summer of 1915 to the spring of 1918, a few weeks on the calendar before Hemingway sailed from New York. In other words, *Farewell* was decidedly not autobiographical. In fact, Hemingway had constructed his novel only after considerable research. He consulted books and almanacs and maps and put these together with his own brief exposure to the war and the yarns he heard from veteran soldiers like his friend Chink Dorman-Smith, working all that into the most historically accurate account he could manage. At no time in Book Three, for instance, does it rain in the novel when it had not actually rained on that day in 1917.

Hemingway was scrupulous about getting the facts right, on the one hand, and was determined, on the other hand, to distance himself from what happened to his protagonist. That distinction is underlined in a long interview that Reynolds conducted with Agnes von Kurowsky, the Red Cross nurse with whom Hemingway fell in love during his recuperation (like Frederic in this case) in the hospital in Milan. The physical setting was meticulously recreated, she acknowledged, but she and Ernest had not been lovers. Certainly the two of them had not run off together to Switzerland. There may be something of Agnes in the portrait of Catherine, but not much, for Hemingway had already laid to rest any such ghost in his 1923 "A Very Short Story." In her total devotion to Frederic, Catherine most resembles Hemingway's first wife Hadley, but in her difficulty giving birth, his second wife Pauline.[31]

Bernard Oldsey's *Hemingway's Hidden Craft: The Writing of "A Farewell to Arms"* (1979) explored the process of composition in still greater detail than had Reynolds. Along with other textual questions, Oldsey focused on the title and the ending. In his worksheets, Hemingway set down thirty-three separate possibilities for a title, almost all of them derived from literary sources, and fifteen of them from *The Oxford Book of English Verse*. Early working titles included *The World's Room* and *In Another Country*, and he apparently did not settle on *A Farewell to Arms* until December 1928. This title stands in ironic counterpoint to its source, George Peele's chivalric poem in which an aging knight regrets that he can no longer serve his queen in battle. And as practically everyone has noticed, it nicely combines Frederic's dual farewell – to the war and to his lover.

Hemingway once said that he had written thirty-nine different endings to *Farewell*, and the manuscripts pretty much bear him out. Oldsey classified these variants into eight different categories – (1) The *Nada* Ending, (2) The Fitzgerald Ending, (3) The Religious Ending, (4) The Live-Baby Ending, (5) The Morning-After Ending, (6) The Funeral Ending, (7) The Original *Scribner's Magazine* Ending, and (8) *The* Ending – and provided examples of each. The *Nada* Ending, for example, reads thus: "That is all there is to the story. Catherine died and you will die and I will die and that is all I can promise you." Fitzgerald had suggested that the novel end with a rhetorical generalization from an earlier chapter to the effect that "the world breaks everyone" and those it does not break it kills: "It kills the very good and the very gentle and the very brave impartially. If you are none of these you can be sure it will kill you too but there will be no special hurry." The serial version concludes with a kind of roundup about what had happened to Rinaldi and Piani and others before moving back to Frederic, waking, alone, in the Lausanne hotel room where he and Catherine had lived. "I could tell about the boy," the Live-Baby Ending begins, but "he does not belong in this story. . . . There is no end except death and birth is the only beginning." Just as bitter is the Funeral Ending: "After people die you have to bury them but you do not have to write about it. . . . In writing you have a certain choice you do not have in life." *Farewell* could hardly have a more perfect ending than the one Hemingway finally chose, but it was not arrived at easily.[32]

In recent years Hemingway often has been the target of feminist critics, and none of them has stated her cause more forcefully than Judith Fetterley in her 1976 essay *"A Farewell to Arms:* Hemingway's 'Resentful Cryptogram'."* Fetterley wondered why it is that the emotional charge of this novel and others on the same theme "so often depends on the death of the woman and so rarely on the death of a man." Behind the idealization of Catherine in *Farewell*, she believes, "is a hostility whose full measure can be taken from the fact that Catherine dies and dies because she is a woman." If we weep at the end, she asserts, it is not for Catherine but for Frederic, because in the novel it is male life that matters. "And the message to women reading this classic love story and experiencing its image of the female ideal is clear and simple: the only good woman is a dead one, and even then there are questions."[33]

Fetterley may have overstated her case; yet her argument depends on a deromanticizing of the love story and a downgrading of Frederic Henry's character that have become critical commonplaces in the last decade and a half. The two lovers do not bear comparison to Romeo and Juliet, for the mentally unstable Catherine commits heresy in her virtual worship of Frederic, and he gives almost nothing of himself to her until it is too late to matter. He is a selfish lover who goes out of his way to absolve himself of even a modicum of guilt for her death. She dies, he tells us, because the world is against them, or because the good die young, or because her hips are too narrow – not because he has impregnated her. Similarly, after diving into the Tagliamento and declaring his separate peace, Frederic adopts a spurious passivity in making his escape. He calculates each step in the process that leads him first to Stresa and then to Switzerland, but constantly pretends that he does not know what to do and must be told by others, who then assume a share of the burden of guilt that is forever dogging this "Anglo-Saxon remorse boy." Surely Frederic is not a self-portrait of the author. Hemingway went out of his way to dissociate himself from his protagonist and also remarked, pointedly, that he was not to be held accountable for the opinions of his narrators. Looked at in one sense, the novel exists only because Frederic felt

20

the need to justify himself, and "the position of the survivor of a great calamity is seldom admirable," as Hemingway wrote on a discarded page of manuscript. Regarded this way, *Farewell* is an *apologia pro vita sua.*[34]

Catherine has been judged more favorably than Frederic in recent criticism. Long regarded as a kind of fantasy woman constructed for little more than the pleasure of Lieutenant Henry, she has increasingly been construed as an admirable person who, though psychologically troubled, is more mature, more loving, and more blessed with a capacity for humor than her lover. In the course of their affair, according to such interpretations, she not only regains her mental health but also is instrumental in teaching Frederic how to love.[35]

The foregoing survey of *Farewell* criticism merely attempts to report on a few of the landmark essays, necessarily omitting many important contributions. It is a novel that invites critical attention. Nearly every year it is the subject of several essays. And, of course, the book is read and taught in thousands of classrooms every semester, and the teachers and students and essayists of today necessarily have a different perspective than those of sixty or thirty or even ten years ago. The new essays collected here represent the most interesting of current studies.

Paul Smith addresses the question of the novel's provenance – how Hemingway came to write *A Farewell to Arms* and why it took him so long – and shows how he was trying out various approaches to the experience of the war in stories and sketches written during the decade between 1918 and 1928. James Phelan examines Hemingway's achievement in creating a complicated yet brilliantly appropriate technique of narration. After reviewing critical attitudes toward Catherine Barkley, Sandra Whipple Spanier concludes that Catherine often has been misunderstood because of lack of awareness of the tensions created by the Great War. Finally, Ben Stoltzfus brings the insights of linguistics and psychoanalysis to bear in a Lacanian reading of the novel. Each of these perspectives – historical-textual, narratological, feminist, psychological – provides a fresh way of looking at a book that has long outlived its time and promises to captivate readers for generations to come.

NOTES

1. For this summary of the composition history of the novel, I am indebted both to Carlos Baker, *Ernest Hemingway: A Life Story* (New York: Scribners, 1969), Chapters 27 and 28, and to Michael S. Reynolds, *Hemingway's First War: The Making of "A Farewell to Arms"* (Princeton, N.J.: Princeton University Press, 1976).

2. Ernest Hemingway to Maxwell Perkins, 16 December 1928, *Ernest Hemingway: Selected Letters 1917–1961*, ed. Carlos Baker (New York: Scribners, 1981), pp. 291–2.

3. Hemingway's correspondence with Scribners in connection with the serialization of *Farewell* is located in the publishing house's files at the Firestone Library of Princeton University. The same collection contains his disclaimer about Italy (in the 26 May 1929 *Salt Lake City Tribune*). Much of this material is included in Michael S. Reynolds, "Words Killed, Wounded, Missing in Action," *Hemingway Notes* 6 (Spring 1981): 2–9.

4. Ernest Hemingway to Maxwell Perkins, 7 June 1929, *Selected Letters*, pp. 296–8. Actually, when *All Quiet on the Western Front* was published by Little, Brown, the American publisher made sixteen deletions from the British edition to soften earthy phrases and dropped two scenes entirely: one set in the camp latrines, and the other describing the carnal reunion of a married soldier and his wife, whom he hasn't seen for two years. See Paul S. Boyer, *Purity in Print: The Vice-Society Movement and Book Censorship in America* (New York: Scribners, 1968), pp. 214–15.

5. The letters of objection from readers of the magazine are preserved in the Scribners files at Princeton.

6. "Boston Police Bar Scribner's Magazine," *New York Times*, 21 June 1929, p. 2.

7. Margaret Getchell Parsons, "Ready to Read," *Worcester Telegram*, 20 October 1929; Boyer, *Purity in Print*, p. 195; Maxwell Perkins to Owen Wister, 8 October 1929, Maxwell Perkins to Ernest Hemingway, 27 June 1929 and 12 July 1929, Scribners files, Princeton.

8. Ernest Hemingway to Maxwell Perkins, 26 July 1929, Maxwell Perkins to Jonathan Cape, 16 August 1929, Scribners files, Princeton.

9. Owen Wister to Maxwell Perkins, 30 April 1929, Maxwell Perkins to Owen Wister, 1 May 1929, Owen Wister to Maxwell Perkins, 6 May 1929, Maxwell Perkins to Ernest Hemingway, 24 May 1929, and Owen Wister to Maxwell Perkins, 14 October 1929, Scribners files, Princeton; Ernest Hemingway to Owen Wister, ca. 25 July 1929,

Selected Letters, p. 301; "Hemingway's Art Matched Only by Defoe's, He Says," *Tulsa Tribune*, 7 July 1929.

10. Reynolds, *Hemingway's First War*, pp. 79–81.

11. James Aswell, *Richmond Times-Dispatch*, 6 October 1929; John Dos Passos, "Books," *New Masses* 5 (1 December 1929): 16, reprinted in *Ernest Hemingway: The Critical Reception*, ed. Robert O. Stephens (New York: Burt Franklin, 1977), p. 95; Clifton P. Fadiman, "A Fine American Novel," *The Nation* 129 (30 October 1929): 497–8, reprinted in Stephens, ed., *Critical Reception*, pp. 83–4; J. B. Priestley, *Now and Then* 34 (Winter 1929): 11–12, reprinted in *Hemingway: The Critical Heritage*, ed. Jeffrey Meyers (London: Routledge & Kegan Paul, 1982), pp. 136–7; Arnold Bennett, *Evening Standard*, 14 November 1929, p. 5, reprinted in Meyers, ed., *Critical Heritage*, pp. 130–1.

12. Fanny Butcher, "Here is Genius, Critic Declares of Hemingway," *Chicago Daily Tribune*, 28 September 1929, p. 11, reprinted in *Critical Reception*, pp. 71–2; Malcolm Cowley, "Not Yet Demobilized," *New York Herald Tribune Books*, 6 October 1929, pp. 1, 6, reprinted in Stephens, ed., *Critical Reception*, pp. 74–6; Henry Hazlitt, "Take Hemingway," *New York Sun*, 28 September 1929, p. 38, reprinted in Stephens, ed., *Critical Reception*, pp. 69–71.

13. Cowley, "Not Yet Demobilized," p. 74; Henry Seidel Canby, "Story of the Brave," *Saturday Review of Literature* 6 (12 October 1929): 231–2, reprinted in Stephens, ed., *Critical Reception*, pp. 78–80.

14. Bernard De Voto, "A Farewell to Arms," *Bookwise* 1 (November 1929): 5–9, reprinted in Meyers, ed., *Critical Heritage*, pp. 85–6; T. S. Matthews, "Nothing Ever Happens to the Brave," *New Republic* 60 (9 October 1929): 208–10, reprinted in Stephens, ed., *Critical Reception*, pp. 76–8; Arnold Bennett, *Evening Standard*, p. 131; Maxwell Perkins to Owen Wister, 17 May 1929, Scribners files, Princeton.

15. See, for example, "Man, Woman, War," *Time* 14 (14 October 1929): 80, reprinted in Stephens, ed., *Critical Reception*, p. 81; Ben Ray Redman, "Spokesman for a Generation," *Spur* 44 (1 December 1929): 77, 186, reprinted in Stephens, ed., *Critical Reception*, p. 97; "Poignant Love Story Told by Ernest Hemingway," *Springfield Republican*, 10 November 1929, p. 4E, reprinted in Stephens, ed., *Critical Reception*, pp. 94–5; Percy Hutchinson, "Love and War in the Pages of Mr. Hemingway," *New York Times Book Review*, 29 September 1929, p. 5, reprinted in Stephens, ed., *Critical Reception*, pp. 72–4.

16. H. L. Mencken, "Fiction by Adept Hands," *American Mercury* 19 (January 1930): 127, reprinted in Stephens, ed., *Critical Reception*, pp. 97–8; Fadiman, "A Fine American Novel," p. 83; Lewis Galantiere, "The

Brushwood Boy at the Front," *Hound and Horn* 3 (January–March 1930): 259–62, reprinted in Meyers, ed., *Critical Heritage,* pp. 101–3.

17. Cowley, "Not Yet Demobilized," p. 75; Henry Seidel Canby, "Chronicle and Comment," *Bookman* 70 (February 1930): 641–7, reprinted in Stephens, ed., *Critical Reception,* pp. 98–100; Reynolds, *Hemingway's First War,* pp. 79–80; Ernest Hemingway to Maxwell Perkins, 30 November 1929, Scribners files, Princeton.

18. For praise of the ending, see the review by Mary Ross, *Survey* 63 (1 November 1929): 166, reprinted in Stephens, ed., *Critical Reception,* p. 90; Ford Madox Ford, "Introduction" to *A Farewell to Arms* (New York: Modern Library, 1932), pp. ix–xx, reprinted in Meyers, ed., *Critical Heritage,* pp. 151–9; Butcher, "Here is Genius," p. 72.

19. Harry Hansen, "The First Reader," *New York World,* 27 September 1929. Although the novel was not legally banned in Boston, either the earlier suppression of *Scribner's Magazine* or some word-of-mouth suggestions to booksellers may have had an effect on sales. Almost every large city in the eastern United States listed it as a best-seller by mid-November, with the exception of Boston: Norman Alexander Hall, "Books and Things," *Town Crier* (Newton, Mass.), 15 November 1929.

20. "What Boston Banned," *Newark News,* 28 September 1929.

21. This summary of objections to the novel is drawn from several sources: John G. Neihardt, "Of Making Many Books," *St. Louis Post-Dispatch,* 30 September 1929; editorial comment in the *Lexington Herald* and *Tulsa World,* both of 1 December 1929: A.C., "Echoes from the Great War in Ernest Hemingway's Novel," *Boston Transcript,* 19 October 1929, Book Section, p. 2, reprinted in Stephens, ed., *Critical Reception,* p. 82.

22. Robert Herrick, "What Is Dirt?" *Bookman* 70 (November 1929): 258–62.

23. Maxwell Perkins to Ernest Hemingway, 19 December 1929, Thornton Wilder to Maxwell Perkins, 2 November 1929, Maxwell Perkins to Owen Wister, 8 November 1929, and Owen Wister to Maxwell Perkins, 12 November 1929, Scribners files, Princeton.

24. Henry Seidel Canby, "Chronicle and Comment," *Bookman* 70 (February 1930): 641–7.

25. Maxwell Perkins to Ernest Hemingway, 19 December 1929, Scribners files, Princeton: M. K. Hare, "Is It Dirt or Is It Art?" *Bookman* 71 (March 1930): xiv–xv, reprinted in Stephens, ed., *Critical Reception,* pp. 100–1.

26. Ford, "Introduction," pp. 151, 156–9.

27. Robert Penn Warren, "Introduction" to *A Farewell to Arms* (New York: Scribners, 1949), pp. vii–xxxvii.

28. Carlos Baker, "The Mountain and the Plain," in *Hemingway: The Writer as Artist* (Princeton, N.J.: Princeton University Press, 1952), pp. 94–109; E. M. Halliday, "Hemingway's Ambiguity: Symbolism and Irony," in *Hemingway: A Collection of Critical Essays*, ed. Robert P. Weeks (Englewood Cliffs, N.J.: Prentice-Hall, 1962), pp. 52–71.

29. Philip Young, *Ernest Hemingway: A Reconsideration* (University Park: Pennsylvania State University Press, 1966), pp. 89–95.

30. Walker Gibson, "The Rhetoric of Frederic Henry," in *Tough, Sweet & Stuffy: An Essay on Modern American Prose Styles* (Bloomington: Indiana University Press, 1966), pp. 28–42.

31. Reynolds, *Hemingway's First War*, throughout.

32. Bernard Oldsey, *Hemingway's Hidden Craft: The Writing of "A Farewell to Arms"* (University Park: Pennsylvania State University Press, 1979).

33. Judith Fetterley, "*A Farewell to Arms:* Hemingway's 'Resentful Cryptogram'," in *The Resisting Reader: A Feminist Approach to American Fiction* (Bloomington: Indiana University Press, 1978), pp. 46–71.

34. For an elaboration of this view of Frederic, see Scott Donaldson, "Frederic Henry, Selfish Lover," in *By Force of Will: The Life and Art of Ernest Hemingway* (New York: Viking Press, 1977), pp. 151–62, and Scott Donaldson, "Frederic Henry's Escape and the Pose of Passivity," in *Hemingway: A Revaluation*, ed. Donald R. Noble (Troy, N.Y.: Whitston, 1983), pp. 165–85.

35. See, among others, Sandra Spanier, "Catherine Barkley and the Hemingway Code: Ritual and Survival in *A Farewell to Arms*," in *Modern Critical Interpretations: A Farewell to Arms*, ed. Harold Bloom (New York: Chelsea, 1987), pp. 131–48; Joyce Wexler, "E.R.A. for Hemingway: A Feminist Defense of *A Farewell to Arms*," *Georgia Review* 35 (1981): 111–23; Roger Whitlow, *Cassandra's Daughters: The Women in Hemingway* (Westport, Conn.: Greenwood Press, 1984), pp. 17–25.

2

The Trying-out of
A Farewell to Arms

PAUL SMITH

S OMETIMES what seems a trivial question can summon up a
complex issue that troubles the placid surface of what we once
thought to be beyond question. As an instance: Why did Ernest
Hemingway write *The Sun Also Rises* (1926) some three years before *A Farewell to Arms* (1929)? Biographers will cite the dramatic
events in the summer of 1925 at the Pamplona festival, the involu-
ted relationships among the coterie of Duff Twysden, Pat Guthrie,
Harold Loeb, and Hemingway himself, as well as his recent discovery of the potential for meaning in the climactic bullfight. All this
offered a novel close to ready-made and certain to stir the social
waters, whether or not it succeeded as a work of fiction. *A Farewell
to Arms* might have been a longer bet.

That makes sense, but there are other, more complex and precise answers to this simple question. Millicent Bell has argued that
A Farewell to Arms, "as a war novel, is curiously late. In 1929,
American society was preoccupied with other things than its
memories" of the war, and Hemingway "had come a long way
from the naive nineteen-year-old of 1918."[1] But however late it
might have been for American society, Hemingway had a larger
audience before him, and it was one that had just acclaimed Erich
Maria Remarque's *All Quiet on the Western Front*.

The novel did come curiously late if one locates its origin in
Hemingway's wounding in July 1918 and his love affair with
Agnes von Kurowsky through the rest of that year. Bell does not
deny the influence of those experiences, but she finds a more
informing source of the novel in the late 1920s: The novel's
"mood and tone, not events, provide unity, and these were more
intensely the concomitants of the present life of the writer than of

27

his younger self. The novel is about neither love nor war; it is about a state of mind, and that state of mind is the author's."[2] Of more moment for her than 1919 are those years of "personal turmoil," from his divorce from Hadley in 1927, through Pauline's pregnancy and the cesarean birth of Patrick, to Ernest's spate of serious accidents – all of them intimating a divinity with a special grudge against Hemingway.[3]

What seems to urge Millicent Bell to underscore the writing of the novel with the immediate life of the writer has less interest for Gerry Brenner in his equally elegant interpretation. Both *The Sun Also Rises* and *A Farewell to Arms* are considered in what he calls the "Thesis Phase" of Hemingway's canon, one marked by two "didactic novels with untrustworthy narrators": first, *A Farewell to Arms,* demonstrating the "conviction that existence is thoroughly irrational," and then *The Sun Also Rises,* implying that one might learn "to live in that irrational world [by joining] discriminating hedonism . . . to vivifying traditions."[4] Brenner assumes that the validity of either thesis does not depend on the narrator's understanding of, or even commitment to, the one novel's desperate vision of existence or the other's tacit response to an irrational world. Rather, it may be that the persuasive force of these novels, more Jamesian than we once thought, depends on their narrators *not* understanding the implications of their narratives. Both Frederic Henry and Jake Barnes say less than they know and, at times, know less than Hemingway wrote.

It is revealing that Brenner takes up these two novels in reverse order – *A Farewell to Arms* first and then *The Sun Also Rises* – for he assumes, as Bell does not, that what engendered Hemingway's novel was, in a sense, there in the more profound events of his early childhood experience with his mother and father; so, although *The Sun Also Rises* was written before *A Farewell to Arms*, in Hemingway's experience the first novel may represent a fictional reaction to the moral issue raised, belatedly perhaps, in the novel that followed it.

Millicent Bell's assumption speaks for a close contemporary source for the novel's mood and tone, the events of 1928, whereas that of Gerry Brenner finds the novel's source some ten or twenty years before that in Hemingway's childhood experience. Either critic's position will seem more persuasive if we accept one or the other's range of relevant evidence. Neither critic would deny the evidence of the other, but each, I am sure, would have strong words to defend the importance of, say, an unpublished manuscript of 1919 compared with that of a story of 1926 or 1927. Bell probably would admit the substantive features of a 1919 manuscript, but would argue that the stylistic features in which those raw details are presented are more significant – her terms, again, are mood and tone. Brenner, as well, would agree that the act of writing brings new experience to bear on old memories, but would be likely to say that the closer the inspiring event to the writer's early experience, the stronger its shaping influence.

I mention these two critics because their differing perspectives question the relevance and influence of Hemingway's published and unpublished writing before he sharpened his pencil and wrote the famous paragraph that begins, "In the late summer of that year we lived in a house in a village that looked across the river and the plain to the mountains" (p. 3). Beyond that, in addressing the trivial question with which we began, they raise a swarm of other questions teeming within the metaphors we use when we speak of the "source" or the "conception" of a novel, as if it arose in some northern headwaters or began on some night of love.

But books are neither rivers nor children. They are words on paper, and the best evidence we have of their origins are similar words on other pages. So to our first question of which novel came first, or should have, in whatever sense we have of the art of writing, we might well consider those published and unpublished words on paper that seem to "predict" – another metaphor – the two novels. And the first fact of the matter is that there are no preliminary fictions, either in manuscript or published, that look forward to *The Sun Also Rises* – with the possible exception of the bullfight chapters of *in our time* – whereas there is a horde of stories and sketches dating from 1919 on that are intimately related to *A Farewell to Arms*. And in these fictions we can witness Hemingway trying out the novel in two ways: trying out in the sense of experimenting with various narrative points of view, differing styles and voices, and here and there selecting one moment or event over another; and also trying out in the sense that

Melville would have understood, reducing the abundant riches of an experience to its essential values. That long process began in Chicago in 1919.

The Chicago Fiction: 1919–21

The earliest manuscript in Hemingway's progress toward the novel is a telling sketch written soon after the armistice in November 1918 on paper bearing an American Red Cross letterhead (KL/EH 604).[5] The narrator recounts a dialogue in which Nick Grainger, lying wounded in a Milan hospital, is talking with a nurse as the sounds of the armistice celebration rise from the streets below. The nurse says that it sounds like a New Year's Eve celebration on Broadway. Nick asks if she is a New Yorker, and she admits she is from Fort Wayne. He recognizes the strategy behind her remark, meant to imply that she was from a cosmopolitan city; and he should know, for he is from Petoskey, Michigan, and confesses, "Sure, I've used that stuff too."

When she leaves, Nick hides a bottle of bichloride of mercury (a common antiseptic, but also a poison) taken from his bedside table and then looks at his war medals and a citation. Each, the medicine and the citation, is a "deadly antiseptic":[6] The bichloride of mercury may help cure a wound, but it could be drunk to commit suicide. The citation is meant to cure with language the wounds he has suffered, but it, too, is rhetorically deadly; for the moment it may gloss his act in the extravagant language of military citations, but later it may remind Nick of the deadly difference between the reality of the act and the words meant to memorialize it.[7]

At the end of the sketch, Nick folds the citation, dismisses it and the medals as a "counterfeit dollar" and a "tin cross," and remarks, "'I had a rendezvous with Death' – but Death broke the date and now it is all over. God double-crossed me." Nick's quotation of Alan Seeger's famous poem, "I Have a Rendezvous with Death," in which the poet forecast his own heroic death, changes the verb's tense from the promissory present to the disgruntled past – the act of a disillusioned romantic.[8] But that simple change of tense also works in an ironic way to deflate the notion of a doomed lover's tryst with Death to that of a schoolboy stood up at the junior prom.

However much that literary allusion may imply, the "cosmopolitan strategy" that Nick and the nurse recognize is more interesting here, for just as the nurse wonders what it is like on Broadway, and Nick catches her out, so Catherine Barkley catches Frederic Henry out in *A Farewell to Arms* when he, not altogether inadvertently, implies that he had witnessed the Battle of the Somme, one of the worst of the war. When she explains that her riding crop "belonged to a boy who was killed last year" (the fall of 1916), he replies,

> "I'm awfully sorry"
> "He was a very nice boy. He was going to marry me and he was killed in the Somme."
> "It was a ghastly show."
> "Were you there?"
> "No." (p. 18)

The line "It was a ghastly show" originally read "It was a terrible show" in the pencil manuscript (KL/EH 64, p. 38), and the revision indicates Hemingway's intention to emphasize that Frederic was affecting a British idiom. The affectation of a characteristically British diction in that line should color our reading of the rest of the wartime courting dialogue when Frederic first meets Catherine. If so, then the reader may ask, as Catherine does, "Were you there?" – not so much for his answer, but to lead to the next obvious question, which she mercifully ignores: "Why, then, did you speak as if you *had* been?"

Although this may be a minor moment in the novel, it leads to larger issues concerning both Hemingway's earlier experience and the fiction that followed. It has become a commonplace for biographers to note the grandiose manner of his homecoming in January 1919. He returned with an abundance of the souvenirs of a returning warrior: the tailored uniform, the flowing cape, the shrapnel-torn breeches, the medals – everything from a star-pistol and shells to a bear-shaped bottle of kümmel. And, as if to authenticate those trophies, he brought back improbable stories of the war: carrying a wounded soldier with his own knee shattered, fighting with the elite Arditi storm troops on Monte Grappa, and being captured for a week in the embraces of a passionate Neapolitan woman.

Tales for the homefolks like these are not unusual among returning soldiers, particularly from those who served on the edges of the action or were in it only by accident. But Hemingway turned some of those tall tales into fiction in the summer and fall of 1919. "The Passing of Pickles McCarty" (or "The Woppian Way") has another Nick, this time Nick Neroni, telling a reporter of leading an Arditi battalion in the attack at Asalone. In "The Mercenaries," a soldier of fortune tells the story of the amorous woman of Naples ensnaring him in a week of love that ends with a Western shoot-out with her husband.[9] Both stories went unpublished – luckily for Hemingway – for the narration, plot, and style all exhibit the desperate exuberance of a young writer eager to win recognition at any cost. Like Frederic Henry with his "ghastly show," the young Hemingway could parrot the diction of the seasoned veteran, and like Nick Grainger, he had reasons later to confess that he, too, had used a veteran's version of the "stuff" of a cosmopolitan strategy.

One other manuscript from this early period shows Hemingway working toward the novel ten years away and showing some sensitivity to the spectrum of language between the romantic and ironic, the idealistic and realistic. "The Visiting Team" opens with a disclaimer of romantic conventions:

> Red Smith lay on a cot, no go on, this is no hospital story. There is no soft-eyed, gentle-voiced nurse, who might have stepped out of the Winter Garden chorus, no romantic young Second Lieutenant romantically wounded through the shoulder. There is not even a Captain with a Croix de Guerre pinned to his pillow, both eyes bandaged while his gruff but tender-hearted Irish orderly – but back to Red who lay on a cot. (KL/EH 670 A, B)[10]

This note of disavowal foreshadows the action of the story. Red Smith, the leader of a veteran ambulance unit, arranges to play a practical joke on some new recruits by simulating a nighttime bombardment with burst light bulbs, pistol shots, and a dusting of chloride of lime. But the joke explodes in their faces with a real attack, the unit going to the front, and Red's fatal wounding. When his ambulance is hit by a shell, he "felt himself floating off into space through a red mist [and coming] back to earth through an endlessness" – the first of several of Hemingway's fictional accounts of his own wounding.[11] As he is dying, he comforts his grieving friend: "'Anyway it's a great war. . . . But only the good die young. . . . It ain't bad. But who would have thought it of the visiting team?' and so passed wonderingly a gentleman unafraid."

That last echo of Kipling suggests that though this may not be a romantic "hospital story," its characters are like the poet's "Gentlemen-rankers out on a spree" who solace themselves with "God help us, for we knew the worst too young!"[12] That sentimental notion that "only the good die young" is no more persuasive here than it is in the novel when Frederic's revery of nights with Catherine is interrupted by the thought that "the world . . . kills the very good and the very gentle and the very brave impartially. If you are none of these you can be sure it will kill you too but there will be no special hurry" (p. 249).

But the story ends with an Italian surgeon, covered with the blood of the dying prankster, asking, Who are the visiting team? The tacit answer, of course, is that they are the enemy, out to kill you, and no metaphor from the playing fields will change that deadly fact.[13]

There are, then, aspects of narrative and style in these early sketches – Red Smith's wounding or Nick Grainger's ironic language dismissing his citation – that inevitably remind us of features in *A Farewell to Arms,* and although they differ in some ways from what Millicent Bell described as the "mood and tone" of the novel originating at the time of its composition, those differences may be more a matter of degree than of kind. In both the early stories and the novel there are moments when the romantic and ironic impulses seem to rest in equilibrium, although the romantic finally dominates the stories, and the novel ends in overwhelming irony. Both Nick Grainger and Frederic Henry imagine a double-crossing divinity, and Red Smith recognizes that the game is for deadly stakes; but the death that is dealt in the stories seems assuaged by the allusions to the bittersweet sentiment of Alan Seeger's poem and Kipling's fiction. When Frederic rages against "the world" that breaks and kills or "they" who catch one off base (pp. 249, 327), he may seem to be invoking Thomas Hardy's "purblind Doomsters";[14] but when the novel ends, not even the solace of an indifferent deity remains.

Nevertheless, the romantic impulse to imagine Frederic and Catherine as "star-crossed lovers" is there in those moments when Frederic tries to make sense, however darkly determined, of Catherine's death. That nothing makes sense of it at the end, not even the telling of the tale, finally stamps that desperate railing against the world and its anonymous powers for what it is – a brief and human clutching at a straw.

Something like this momentary impulse toward the romantic is evident in the novel's manuscript itself. In the celebrated passages in which Frederic disavows those "abstract words such as glory, honor, courage, or hallow [that] were obscene beside the concrete names of villages," Hemingway originally cited an exception: "the only things glorious were the cavalry riding with lances" (p. 184; KL/EH 64, p. 355). He quickly crossed out the line, for the image of glorious lancers calls to mind the romance of chivalry and its assumptions – but for the moment he meant it.[15]

Another similarity between these stories and the novel lies in the imagery of sports and games: Nick Neroni trades boxing for derring-do, the Austrians are the visiting team, and other stories of this period focus on sports and sportsmen. In the novel, of course, there is also a pattern of sporting and gaming imagery. That characters engage in, or gamble on, sports may or may not be innocent of meaning; here, the occasions of, or allusions to, hunting and fishing, luge-ing, boxing, and even billiards with Count Greffi are, by and large, simple acts or references with little more than ordinary meaning. But as Robert W. Lewis has shown in an essay on "Soldier's Home," characters may reach out to a game for its "uncomplicated world [of rules that are] purely arbitrary and gratuitous and without pretense to meaning or significance outside themselves,"[16] to grasp for patterns that, in a way, offer order without the burden of meaning or moral commitment. And that may account for several of the sporting references in the novel. More interesting in that pattern of images are those few instances in which some moral aspect of a sporting event is engaged: first, to say something of the characters' experience, as when Frederic and Catherine fail to win big on a crooked horse race, and then bet on a sure loser that finished fourth in a field of five – something like a sporting act of contrition (pp. 130–1); second, to afford the characters themselves the chance to order and inform their actions with metaphors from games or sports. Early on in the novel, Frederic sees all the moves in his courtship as moves in a chess game, or a game of bridge with unforeseen stakes; and then Catherine, as if reading his mind, remarks that "this is a rotten game we play" (pp. 26, 30, 31). The hidden stakes in such seemingly innocent conversation rise to relevance when Frederic "dropped one" of the two sergeants in the engineers, as if that soldier were a duck (p. 204). Finally, in Frederic's penultimate attempt to explain Catherine's imminent death to himself, he imagines our destiny as if we were kids in a sandlot baseball game: "They threw you in and told you the rules and the first time they caught you off base they killed you," or for sideliners like Aymo, "they killed you gratuitously" (p. 327). To realize the rules of *this* ballgame – that when you are out, you are really out – is to recognize the implication of Red Smith's dying remark: "Who would have thought it of the visiting team?"

But Hemingway must have known that even that realization could leave its victims with the sense that, whatever their fates, there *were* rules, however final. So he added that they can kill "you gratuitously like Aymo"; and it is that remark that leads to the recollection of ants burning on a campfire log, with a camper as messiah manqué, who saves them from the fire to steam them to death only because he wants to empty his tin cup (pp. 327–8). With that exemplum we are left with nothing, not even the solace of a malign deity who abrogates the rules that were never rules in the first place.

The Paris Fiction: 1922–4

Ernest and Hadley came to Paris in December 1921 with rather light literary baggage. Hemingway must have known that the likes of Gertrude Stein and Ezra Pound would have little interest in the sort of popular fiction he had written in Chicago; so he left it there. And a year later, in early December 1922, as if chance meant to confirm his judgment, all but a few of his manuscripts were stolen from Hadley in the Gare de Lyon as she entrained to meet him in Switzerland.

But he had earlier set himself the regimen he later described in *A Moveable Feast*, beginning with "one true sentence" and then going on to "paragraphs that would be the distillation of what made a novel,"[17] and by the early winter of 1923 he was at work on those paragraphs that became the chapters of the Paris *in our time* (1924) and were later included in the first major collection of his stories, *In Our Time* (1925). There are some eight of those brief chapters that, if not distillations of *A Farewell to Arms*, seem like preliminary sketches for scenes or motifs in the novel.

In Chapter I the narrator tells of a whole artillery battery drunk as they march "along the road in the dark . . . to the Champagne," where in the late fall of 1915 some 300,000 French and Germans were killed. At the end he recalls that "it was funny going along that road," and as if to justify that remark given the slaughter he must have witnessed, "that was when I was a kitchen corporal" (*Short Stories*, p. 89). This may recall the boyish behavior in "The Visiting Team," but it also looks toward some of the more vinous scenes in the novel.

The description in the novel of the peasants retreating before the Austrians after Caporetto drew its details from Chapter II of *in our time* and the *Toronto Daily Star* dispatch from which it in turn was derived. Compare, for example, "Women and kids were in the carts crouched with mattresses, mirrors, sewing machines, bundles" in the chapter (*Short Stories*, p. 97) with "There were mirrors projecting up between mattresses, and . . . there was a sewing machine on the cart ahead of us in the rain" (p. 198).

In Chapter VI, Nick is wounded in the spine, with his "legs stuck out awkwardly." He turns to his companion Rinaldi and says, "you and me we've made a separate peace" (*Short Stories*, p. 139), like the separate peace Frederic proclaims, without his companion Rinaldi, on his way to Stresa to join Catherine[18] (p. 243).

The soldier terrified under the bombardment in Chapter VII prays to his savior, "Dear jesus please let me out. Christ please please please Christ. If you'll only keep me from getting killed I'll do anything you say" (*Short Stories*, p. 143), as Frederic does when Catherine's condition becomes critical: "Dear God, don't let her die. Please, please, please don't let her die. . . . I'll do anything you say if you don't let her die" (p. 330). Whether or not the prayer worked for the soldier, he forgot his promise to tell the whole world that Christ is "the only one that matters," not even the "girl he went upstairs with at the Villa Rossa." And the chapter, like the novel with its priest and another Villa Rossa, sets the spirit and the flesh, sacred and profane love, in dramatic opposition.

In three chapters, one unpublished, Hemingway explored the dramatic possibilities of a narrative voice, probably modeled on that of his friend from 1918 on, Chink Dorman-Smith. Chapters III and IV are set at Mons, where Dorman-Smith served during the German attack and the British retreat in August 1914. In Chapter III, a British officer tells of young Buckley returning from patrol, and then the way they "potted" German soldiers climbing over a garden wall, and notices that they "looked awfully surprised." But a serious note infects this narration when the chapter ends with this quiet remark: "We shot them. They all came just like that" (*Short Stories*, p. 105). In the next chapter, the narrator's delight in having set up "an absolutely perfect barricade, . . . simply price-less, . . . absolutely topping," diminishes at the chapter's end when he notes that "we were frightfully put out when we heard the flank had gone, and we had to pull out" (*Short Stories*, p. 113). In the last unpublished chapter of this set (KL/EH 94 A), the narrator (now named Charles) and Buckley are forming the Gordon Highlanders for the retreat, and the soldiers move out before the order to march is given. Charles notices with admiration that the men had fought well, kept "all together and they still had their rifles"; but Buckley is furious at the breach of discipline: "'It's no good Charles,' Buckley said. His face was red and he sounded sick. It wasn't at all like Sandhurst."[19]

Together the three chapters form a dialectic drama that rises through the first to a height of elation in the second and ends in the third with the quiet irony of the chastened narrator recognizing, as young Buckley does not, the contrast between the discipline of a retreat in a military textbook and the discipline of defeat on a battlefield. Carlos Baker is surely right that Hemingway "admired and sought to imitate" Dorman-Smith's "clipped British fashion" of speaking,[20] but the question raised is to what literary purposes Hemingway put that talent for mimicry. In these three chapters, the evident motive is to dramatize the narrator's growing perception that there is no such thing as an absolutely perfect barricade; that those fine enemy officers he so sportingly potted were, in fact, shot; and at last that the language of absolutes – perfect, priceless, topping – is as obscene as the language of abstractions – sacred, glorious, and sacrifice – would become for Frederic Henry.

The relationship between "A Very Short Story," originally chapter 10 of *in our time*, and the novel presents a special, and celebrated, case for criticism. The most revised of all the chapters, and one of the two to achieve the status of a story, it has either a little or a lot to do with *A Farewell to Arms*, depending on one's critical persuasion. Relatively few of the story's details, and only those in the first three paragraphs, reappear with some revision in the novel. The narrator tells of the two lovers, a wounded soldier and his nurse Ag, watching the searchlights from the roof of a hospital in Milan (Padua in the *in our time* version, and she is named Luz). She takes night duty to be with him and prepares him with an enema for his operation; he tries to keep from revealing their intimacy under anesthesia. Later, on crutches, he takes the temperatures of the few other patients so that she can sleep. Before he returns to the front, they pray in the Duomo, and although they want to marry and want others to know it, there is no time for it. Most of these details, with some variation, appear in Chapters XVI–XVIII of the novel (pp. 102, 103, 107, 108, 113, 115).

But nothing in the rest of the short story appears in the novel. At its center, the fourth paragraph, he reads her love letters, which have been delayed until the armistice. In the fifth paragraph they agree to part, he to return to the States, and she to follow once he has a job and has given up drinking, but they quarrel when he leaves. In the sixth paragraph she has an affair with a major in the Arditi whom she plans to marry, and she writes to her onetime lover to tell him that although she loved him, theirs was only a "boy and girl love." In the last paragraph, her marriage is called off, and he contracts gonorrhea from a salesgirl in Chicago (*Short Stories*, pp. 141–2).

Every biographer since Carlos Baker in 1969 has remarked on the autobiographical nature of the story, and some have used the story to document their biographies. Others have reasoned from this evidence, that because the last half of the story has *no* explicit parallel in the novel, there must be some radical relationship between the end of the story, in life and fiction, and the end of the novel, one probably accessible through psychological criticism.

Various critics have noted that beneath the story's sardonic narration, beginning ironically at the "armistice," there are intimations of a deep anger, almost malice, in the authorial voice; and that may argue for the near identity, even without the biographical evidence, among Hemingway, the narrator, and the soldier – so, in Robert Scholes's terms, "something punitive is going on here, as the discourse seems to be revenging itself on the character" of Luz.[21]

From there it is a short step (although a long decade in Hemingway's life) to conclude that Catherine's fated "rendezvous with death" was an act of revenge for Agnes's failure to keep her rendezvous with Ernest. If so, then "A Very Short Story" of a very short affair has much more to do with the novel than do any of the other *in our time* chapters.[22]

In late August 1923, Hemingway had the eighteen chapters ready for the Paris *in our time* volume, and he and Hadley left for Toronto and the birth of their son. They endured five months there, returning to Paris in January 1924, and that marked the beginning of Hemingway's miraculous year: During that year he wrote twelve stories, eight of them by May 1924.

One of the best of those eight was "Soldier's Home," a story of a veteran home from the wars that darkens the once-bright souvenirs of Hemingway's triumphant return in January 1919. It is divided into two equal sections: first, a discursive portrait of the veteran Harold Krebs, recounting some of his service – he enlisted in the Marines in 1917, fought from Belleau Wood to the Argonne through the summer of 1918, and after the armistice was stationed on the Rhine – but much more of his troubled attempts to return to the routines and values of life at home. The second is a morning's dialogue, first with his favorite sister Helen, something of a tomboy, and then with his well-meaning but tiresome mother. She calls up all the stale middle-class values of work and home and marriage to encourage him to settle down, get a job, and date nice girls; then,

> "Is that all?" Krebs said.
> "Yes. Don't you love your mother, dear boy?"
> "No," Krebs said. (*Short Stories*, pp. 151–2)

The scene ends with the two kneeling, but only his mother can pray.

Krebs cannot or will not tell her what troubles him; so we are returned to the earlier omniscient portrait for some explanation. By the time Krebs had returned home "years after the war was over [the] town had heard too many atrocity stories to be thrilled by actualities [and he] found that to be listened to at all he had to lie."[23]

> His lies were quite unimportant lies and consisted in attributing to himself things other men had seen, done or heard of, and stating as facts certain apocryphal events familiar to all soldiers. . . . Krebs acquired the nausea in regard to experience that is the result of untruth or exaggeration, and when he occasionally met another man who had really been a soldier . . . he fell into the easy pose of the old soldier among other soldiers: that he had been badly, sickeningly frightened all the time. In this way he lost everything. (*Short Stories*, p. 145)

At first Krebs fails the homefolks by refusing to draw on apocryphal stories of atrocities rather than the actualities of his own experience, and then later he betrays *himself* by doing so. Among his losses is the inner pride he felt when he thought of "the times so long back when he had done one thing, the only thing for a man to do, easily and naturally, when he might have done something else" (*Short Stories*, pp. 145–6). The sentence is a curious circumlocution for the words "bravery" and "cowardice," but what it implies is that even the actualities of his experience have become infested by his lies.

That is a serious condition, an existential nausea that Krebs's family, of all people, can hardly comprehend. His only recourse lies in his dispassionate observation of patterns: those patterns in the photograph of himself "among his fraternity brothers, all of them wearing exactly the same height and style collar," and those among the girls who "all wore sweaters and shirt waists with round Dutch collars" (*Short Stories*, pp. 145, 147), and, finally, those patterns that govern sports, the rules of the game that have their appeal, as Robert Lewis said, simply because they are arbitrary, gratuitous, and without meaning once the game is over (see note 18).

Krebs's condition was certainly not unusual; it was, rather, almost epidemic among those who came of cannon-fodder age in 1914, and in generations since then. In *Exile's Return*, Malcolm Cowley, one of Hemingway's contemporaries, wrote of their generation's colossal indifference toward the social morality that valorized war; and with a certain logic he argued that although such indifference "might have been learned in any branch of the army, the ambulance service had a lesson of its own: it instilled into us what might be called the *spectatorial* attitude."[24] That is the perfect term, for the common meaning of a "spectator" is someone watching a game.

Krebs's case is severe: He cannot lie about loving his mother as Frederic Henry, at least early on, can about loving Catherine. Yet the two men are more alike than not, for Krebs shares both what Millicent Bell identifies as Frederic's "affectlessness" or "dryness of soul," expressed in a language of "alienated neutrality," and what Gerry Brenner calls his "illusion of self-sufficiency" and "regressive withdrawal from reality."[25]

One last, and perhaps the most significant, interest in patterns that Krebs and Frederic share is revealed in their reading: For Krebs it is recent histories

> about all the engagements he had been in. It was the most interesting reading he had ever done. . . . He looked forward with a good feeling to reading all the really good histories when they would come out with good detail maps. Now he was really learning about the war. He had been a good soldier. That made a difference. (*Short Stories*, p. 148)

For Frederic it is the newspapers: When he has the chance in Milan before his operation, during his recuperation, and later at Stresa and in Switzerland, he turns first to the papers for the war news (pp. 95, 136, 292, 308, 329). And the details of the war, as

41

Michael Reynolds demonstrated, "could be no more accurate than if they were in a military history, which is where Hemingway very likely found many of them."[26]

Krebs's interest in detailed battle maps is reflected in perhaps the most familiar passage in all of Hemingway's work, Frederic's musing on the proclamations of the patriotic:

> I was always embarrassed by the words sacred, glorious, and sacrifice and the expression in vain. We had heard them, sometimes standing in the rain almost out of earshot, so that only the shouted words came through, and had read them, on proclamations that were slapped up by billposters over other proclamations, now for a long time, and I had seen nothing sacred, and the things that were glorious had no glory and the sacrifices were like the stockyards at Chicago if nothing was done with the meat except to bury it. There were many words that you could not stand to hear and finally only the names of places had dignity. Certain numbers were the same way and certain dates and these with the names of the places were all you could say and have them mean anything. Abstract words such as glory, honor, courage, or hallow were obscene beside the concrete names of villages, the numbers of roads, the names of rivers, the numbers of regiments and the dates. (pp. 184–5)

The names of villages and rivers, the numbers of regiments and roads, and the dates are all, and are *only*, recorded in the detailed historical maps of battles. They are, of course, no more concrete or less abstract than words like "sacred" or "glory," but they are particular, specific, precise – and imposed upon the topography of a place, they mark its identity and significance in a moment of history, they give it a pattern. And for both Krebs and Frederic, "that made a difference."

The Early "Chapters": 1925–6

From the early winter of 1925 to the fall of 1926, Hemingway tried twice to approach *A Farewell to Arms* through the form of a story. On 15 April 1925, in his first letter to Maxwell Perkins, he confessed that he thought the novel "to be an awfully artificial and worked out form but as some of the short stories now are stretching out . . . maybe I'll get there yet."[27] The first try probably was made between December 1924 and February 1925 and then abandoned in manuscript – it has since been published by Bernard Oldsey as "The Original Beginning."[28] It begins as a story of a wounded soldier, Emmett Hancock, arriving at a Milan hospital, and after the first day it continues as "Chapter Two." Hemingway had it in hand to revise as Chapter XIII of *A Farewell to Arms* in early June 1928.

In September 1926 he may have tried again with "In Another Country," the first of his published Italian war stories. Julian Smith has argued that the similarities between it and the novel could have qualified it as a chapter in *A Farewell to Arms* inserted after Chapter XVIII or XX.[29] And somewhat like "The Original Beginning," which grew from a sketch to include a second chapter, "In Another Country" was followed by "Now I Lay Me" in November 1926, the working title for which was "In Another Country – Two" through early 1927. [It is something of a curiosity that when *A Farewell to Arms* was first translated into German in 1930, it bore the title *In einem andern Land* (*In Another Country*) and the epigraph quotation from Christopher Marlowe's *The Jew of Malta*, which was its source.[30]]

"The Original Beginning" is an intriguing manuscript in itself as well as in its relationship to *A Farewell to Arms*. Told from the third-person point of view (rather than the first person of the novel), it recounts Lt. Emmett Hancock's arrival by ambulance at a hospital in Milan, his awkward and painful ascent to the fourth floor by elevator, the confusion that his unexpected arrival causes the nurse on duty (Mrs. Walker, as in the novel), and finally his tipping the Italians and turning over his papers to the nurse before he goes to sleep. In Chapter Two, he wakes to find an attractive American nurse who takes his temperature and, with another nurse, bathes him and cleans all but his head wound, apparently his most serious. All these details appear in the opening pages of Chapter XIII in the novel (pp. 81–6).

Two elements, however, do not appear in the novel. The first element is the pain Hancock suffers in several passages where Hemingway seems to be trying out metaphors to capture the experience: It is likened to "dropping in an elevator" and to a coldness "far inside between the bones" and "going back and forth from the flesh into the bone" or "up and down like a fever chart" (KL/EH

240). (Although this fixation on pain may have been inappropriate for the more stoic Frederic Henry, a similar passage found its way into the novel's manuscript just after Frederic's operation.[31]) The second element occurs in a passage just after Hancock has been bathed, an experience he finds embarrassing but "pleasant" (Hemingway first wrote "exciting"), because no woman, except for his mother, nurse, and sisters when young, had ever seen him naked. With no control over his sphincter muscle, he has been unable to move his bowels for a week; but then four times he defecates in his bed and has to be washed and given a rubber sheet, making him feel "less like an officer [and gentleman]."

Hancock's fixation on his pain and his infantile helplessness reveal Hemingway's conception of a character quite different from Frederic Henry. Hancock is much younger, less stoic, and less worldly than Frederic; still, he is more like Frederic than like that young cynic, Nick Grainger, or the dashing figures of the Chicago fiction. However, his excruciating pain and his embarrassing incontinence do more than signify Hancock's relative youthfulness, for they show Hemingway coming closer to the detailed actualities of war, at least to those of the unmanning helplessness of the wounded, an approach that had begun with the writing of the *in our time* chapters.

The penultimate page of "The Original Beginning" ends with an unfinished paragraph that turns to Hancock's recollection that "he had not wanted to leave the hospital at the front. He had not wanted to come back to Milan except for the nurses. . . . He had wanted one to fall in love with. But these had not attracted him, instead they" – and we might complete the sentence with "were too old, like Mrs. Walker," and (to repeat an earlier sentence from that page) "all he did was ruin bedsheets and have to be looked after like a baby." (In both "A Very Short Story" and the novel, the patient and the nurse become lovers before she gives him an enema.)

This paragraph was immediately deleted, and so it contributes less than one might wish to the question of Hemingway's earliest conception of the novel's plot – that is, if he had one. It could suggest that Hemingway intended to begin *in medias res*, assuming that the things he would begin in the middle of were the events of the finished novel, by returning later to recount the story of his wounding; or he may have meant to begin the story with Hancock's recuperation and meeting a nurse "to fall in love with," and thereby avoid the difficulties of re-creating the retreat from Caporetto from his reading.[32]

"The Original Beginning" ends with a single page recollecting a soldier's days in a hospital at the front. This last page has the independent unity and dramatic power of some of the *in our time* chapters. It begins with two seemingly contradictory sentences: "When he shut his eyes he could see the hospital at the front. He could see it with his eyes open." Then there is a description of a hospital orderly fashioning a brush from newspaper strips to whisk the flies from the wounded man, followed by his being carried out to have his wounds dressed and then returned to a newly made bed. This much was incorporated in the opening paragraph of the novel's Chapter X. But it ends with an image more shocking and ironic than anything Hemingway ever wrote of war, and more so than anything in *A Farewell to Arms:*

> At night no one could sleep and you all sang. When your orderly went to sleep in the daytime [the] and stopped brushing away the flies they settled on your face if you were asleep and left things in the corners of your eyes, ⟨and⟩ in your nose. [and] The doctor swabbed them out with [a] cotton on a stick. The doctor said that since the dead had been buried and the Piave cleaned up after the offensive the flies would try and lay eggs anywhere.

Like the bone-deep pain and the fouled sheets, this image of the flies of war deprived of their dead and settling to generate on the eyes of the sleeping wounded is left out of the novel.

But its memory may still have been there, for Hemingway wrote Chapter XIII of the novel with that conclusion of his earlier version before him. That version ended on page 6 with the phrase "try and lay eggs anywhere" inserted in a smaller script at the bottom, and following the last manuscript page (197) of the novel's Chapter XIII is a page numbered 7 with only those last five horrifying words on it, left like the things the flies left – anywhere. When

Hemingway wrote the last page of Chapter XIII, Frederic is about to go to sleep after nearly finishing a bottle of vermouth:

> Afterward it was dark outside and I could see the beams of the searchlights moving in the sky. I watched for a while and then went to sleep. I slept heavily except once I woke sweating and scared and then went back to sleep trying to stay outside of my dream. (p. 88)

This is the first and only night that Frederic is awakened by a terrifying dream, one to stay outside of, one in which he might have relived his wounding, but more likely dreamt of those flies at work when one slept in a field hospital near the Piave now cleared of its dead.

With *The Sun Also Rises* happily completed and his marriage to Hadley unhappily ended by the early summer of 1926, Hemingway entered another dry spell; but by August it was broken with the writing of "A Canary for One," his hail and farewell to Hadley, and he turned in September and November to the writing of "In Another Country" and "Now I Lay Me." Both stories associate the consequences of a failed or tragically sundered marriage, perhaps called to mind by the sad separation in "A Canary for One," with the war and wounding. In "Now I Lay Me," the first story to introduce, some eight years after the version in "The Visiting Team," the traumatic effects of a wounding, the overpowering subject is Nick's recollection of his parents' perfect union of cruelty and complacency. "In Another Country" brings together the variety of the wounded's agonies and the major's bitter loss of his wife; but of the two stories it is by far the more important in Hemingway's long and deliberate approach to *A Farewell to Arms*.

It is true, as Julian Smith noted, that this story shares with the novel more elements of character and scene than does any other story. The narrator is a wounded American who visits a Milan hospital for mechano-therapy on a severe wound in his lower leg and knee. Although, like his fellow-wounded, he considers his wound an accident, he feels different from all but one of the others because his medals were awarded largely because he was an American. He is neither unafraid of dying nor brave at the thought of returning to the front, and he notices that however "patriotic" the café girls at the Cova, in the communist parts of town the people revile him as an officer. These political and social antagonisms are reflected in the conversations of the ambulance drivers in the novel, as all the other elements are incorporated in passing through the novel (see especially pp. 113, 117, 119, 121, 148).

But all these shared features of the story and novel are mere details next to the dramatic relationship between the story's narrator and the major, once a champion fencer, but now with an irreparably wounded and withered hand, and its relevance to the novel. The two characters share something of the tutor-and-tyro or master-and-apprentice relationship familiar to Hemingway readers since Earl Rovit's original study in 1962.[33] The story's narrator (often taken as Nick Adams, or like him) is not married, but hopes to be on his return to the States – shades of "A Very Short Story," and, of course, the novel. But the major, who knows that his own young wife is dying of pneumonia, angrily tells the narrator that "a man must not marry. . . . If he is to lose everything, he should not place himself in a position to lose that. . . . He should find things that he cannot lose" (*Short Stories*, p. 271).

Had this story been inserted as something of a "chapter" in the novel, it would have foreshadowed the novel's conclusion and made redundant Catherine's own dark intuitions of her death. More than that, the major's desperate counsel would have echoed in the reader's mind just at the moment when Frederic Henry predicates some of the conditions on which he makes his "separate peace," declaring that "I was not made to think. I was made to eat. My God, yes. Eat and drink and sleep with Catherine" (pp. 233, 243). What wet and hungry man riding on a flatcar and long gone from his beloved would not have said this? But abstracted in the thematic progression of the novel, it is more than an occasional remark. Philosophers might mark it as an instance of the "hedonistic paradox": that although the hedonist should seek only pleasure, if pleasure is the only object sought, it cannot be found. And we might note that if Frederic is more than daydreaming, he has settled for things of the flesh and is doomed to witness their evanescence.

That is what the major of "In Another Country," tortured by his wife's impending death, so vehemently proclaims to the young narrator who hopes to be married. And if that is the burden of the story and later of the novel, it is certainly the last council of the hopeless – one that confirms Gerry Brenner's argument that the novel construes "existence as thoroughly irrational" and Frederic Henry as close to suicide. But if that is not the last word of the story, it is also conceivably not the last word in the novel. Two critics' commentaries on the story raise those questions. Arthur Waldhorn said of the story that although there is little overt evidence that the major's outburst has had any impact on the narrator, its "power emerges . . . in the significant details [he] records," and, finally, that what the reader perceives is what the narrator learns: "settling for what cannot be lost excludes love" – and, we may add, almost everything else we yearn for.[34]

Colin Cass is the other critic whose reading of the story raises a question about the novel. In some ways the story's narrator is like Frederic Henry: He is narrating the story long after its events, as Frederic Henry may be.[35] What Cass demonstrated is that the story is a drama of perception, enacted in the narrator's perception of the major and, beyond that, the major's perception of – for want of a better term – reality. After the first celebrated paragraph of the story, we readers watch the narrator watching the major looking where? At false photographs, at a blank wall, at a useless machine, through the window, or at nothing? (*Short Stories*, pp. 268–72). The obvious irrelevance of the photographs, the futility of the machines, and the utter blankness of the major's vision of the empty window and, finally, nothing – all these suggest that he, at least, has recognized the consequences of his passionate commitment to "things he cannot lose." The narrator of the story does not indicate that he is aware of the moral consequences of either the major's desperate advice or his vision of human triviality or ultimate nothingness.

So the first question this story asks is close to one of the final questions we must ask of the novel. What, at the end, does Frederic Henry perceive, and what is he able to learn from another person's perception of events? With "In Another Country," Hemingway tried out the drama of an innocent narrator witnessing the agony of an older and wiser man not only suffering the loss of his beloved but also "looking" at the empty world that has been left him. And perhaps the last question it asks us to consider in the novel is whether or not in the writing of *A Farewell to Arms* Hemingway was able to temper the apparent innocence of the narrator of "In Another Country" with the cold cynicism of the major to complete the character of Frederic Henry, for he begins as something of an innocent, and in the telling of the tale he not only relives the inevitable outcome of loving another person but also learns at last how that love instructs us to bear its loss.

Looking back now through this decade of his fiction, it seems that among the more complex answers to our original question – Why did Hemingway write *A Farewell to Arms* after *The Sun Also Rises?* – there may be another tentative answer: He didn't. It seems now that he began *A Farewell to Arms* in 1919, and it took him ten years to get it right, to try it out.

NOTES

1. Millicent Bell, "*A Farewell to Arms:* Pseudoautobiography and Personal Metaphor," in *Ernest Hemingway: The Writer in Context,* ed. James Nagel (Madison: University of Wisconsin Press, 1984), p. 119.
2. Bell, "Pseudoautobiography," p. 111.
3. Bell, "Pseudoautobiography," p. 119.
4. Gerry Brenner, *Concealments in Hemingway's Works* (Columbus: Ohio State University Press, 1983), p. 4. Perhaps the first irrational aspect of *A Farewell to Arms* is Frederic Henry's assumption that the world could or should be rational, and that of *The Sun Also Rises* is the sentimental notion that either Brett Ashley's or Jake's own hedonism can be wed to the vivifying traditions of the Spaniards – which is not to deny these conceptions as theses, but simply to note their inadequacy.
5. Items in the John F. Kennedy Library's Hemingway collection (KL/EH, with item number) refer to the *Catalog of the Ernest Hemingway Collection at the John F. Kennedy Library* (Boston: G. K. Hall & Co., 1982). Hemingway's deletions are indicated with square brackets, [ ], and his additions with angle brackets, ⟨ ⟩.
6. This analysis is from my article "Hemingway's Apprentice Fiction: 1919–1921," *American Literature* 58 (1986): 574–88.
7. The language of Grainger's citation is close to that of Hemingway's own, reprinted in Robert W. Lewis, "Hemingway in Italy: Making It Up," *Journal of Modern Literature* 9 (1981–2): 22–4.
8. In "Hemingway's Apprentice Fiction," p. 581, I suggest that the poet "was more important to Hemingway than the poem. Seeger, Harvard

class of 1910, resident of Greenwich Village and Paris, and a true mercenary with the Foreign Legion, wrote his famous poem and died in France when Hemingway was trying out for the Junior Varsity" in 1916.

9. Michael Reynolds paraphrased the first in *The Young Hemingway* (Oxford: Basil Blackwell, 1986), pp. 58–9; Peter Griffin published the second in *Along With Youth* (Oxford University Press, 1985), pp. 104–12.

10. In the novel, Catherine confesses to "having a silly idea [that her fiancé] might come to the hospital where I was. With a sabre cut, I suppose, and a bandage around his head. Or shot through the shoulder. Something picturesque" (p. 20).

11. Leicester Hemingway recalled his brother saying of his wounding that "it seemed as I were moving off somewhere in a red din. I said to myself, 'Gee! Stein, you're dead,' and then I began to feel myself pulling back to earth." *My Brother, Ernest Hemingway* (New York: Fawcett World Library, 1963), p. 47. The similarity between the "red mist" of the story and the "red din" of the recollection may be persuasive if one ignores the facts that Leicester was four at the time and the memoir was published two years after Ernest's death.

12. Rudyard Kipling, "Gentlemen-Rankers."

13. Hemingway wrote to Max Perkins in 1942: "I was an awful dope when I went to the last war. . . . I can remember just thinking that we were the home team and the Austrians were the visiting team." Quoted in Carlos Baker, *Ernest Hemingway: A Life Story* (New York: Scribners, 1969), p. 38.

14. Thomas Hardy, "Hap."

15. The image crosses Nick's mind, curiously, at the end of the last war story, "A Way You'll Never Be": "They had once passed the Terza Savoia cavalry regiment riding in the snow with their lances. The horses' breath made plumes in the cold air." *The Short Stories of Ernest Hemingway* (New York: Scribners, 1938), p. 414, hereafter cited as *Short Stories* in the text.

16. "Hemingway's Concept of Sport and 'Soldier's Home'," *Rendezvous* 5 (Winter 1970): 24–5.

17. *A Moveable Feast* (New York: Scribners, 1964), pp. 12, 75. It may be that the "Paris 1922" sentences remain as evidence of that discipline; they are reprinted in Baker, *Ernest Hemingway: A Life Story*, pp. 90–1.

18. E. R. Hagemann points out that in the 1924 *in our time*, Rinaldi's name is Rinaldo Rinaldi, "A Collation, with Commentary, of the Five Texts of the Chapters in Hemingway's *In Our Time*, 1923–38," in

Critical Essays on Hemingway's In Our Time, ed. Michael S. Reynolds (Boston: G. K. Hall & Co., 1983). That name, incidentally, inverts the name of the narrator in "The Mercenaries."

19. Paul Smith, "'Mons (Three)': An Unpublished *In Our Time* Chapter," in *Hemingway in Italy and Other Essays*, ed. Robert W. Lewis (New York: Praeger, 1990).

20. Baker, *Ernest Hemingway: A Life Story*, p. 53.

21. Robert Scholes's chapter, "Decoding Papa: 'A Very Short Story' as Work and Text," in *Semiotics and Interpretation* (New Haven: Yale University Press, 1982), is the most recent and interesting of the studies of this aspect of the story.

22. On the character of Catherine and the implications of her death, see Judith Fetterley, *The Resisting Reader: A Feminist Approach to American Fiction* (Bloomington: Indiana University Press, 1978), and James Phelan, *Reading People, Reading Plots: Character, Progression, and the Interpretation of Narrative* (University of Chicago Press, 1989).

23. Hemingway has Krebs returning in the summer of 1919, hardly "years after the war was over"; in the original manuscript the year was 1920, but that was changed, creating the inconsistency.

24. Malcolm Cowley, *Exile's Return: A Literary Odyssey of the 1920s* (New York: Viking Press, 1951), p. 38.

25. Bell, "Pseudoautobiography," p. 112; Brenner, *Concealments*, p. 41.

26. Michael S. Reynolds, *Hemingway's First War: The Making of "A Farewell to Arms"* (Princeton, N.J.: Princeton University Press, 1976), p. 103. This book, to whose author my indebtedness is obvious and long-standing, is the first to which the student should turn, for Reynolds was the first to discover the sources of the novel in Hemingway's reading, as well as the first to draw the lines of similarity among Harold Krebs, Frederic Henry, and Hemingway himself.

27. *Ernest Hemingway: Selected Letters 1917–1961*, ed. Carlos Baker (New York: Scribners, 1981), p. 156.

28. Bernard Oldsey, *Hemingway's Hidden Craft: The Writing of "A Farewell to Arms"* (University Park: Pennsylvania State University Press, 1979), pp. 93–9. The date of composition of "The Original Beginning" in the early months of 1925 is speculative. Oldsey argues that the two chapters were written in 1919, but the style is more mature than that of the Chicago fiction and closer to that of the *in our time* chapters of 1923. It is possible that it was written soon after January 1924, when Hemingway returned to Paris from Toronto with the war sketches of *in our time* in mind as a model. And for all its similarity in plot to Chapter XIII of the novel, the dissimilarities between the characters of

Hancock and Henry argue that this beginning was not composed in
the early months of 1928. But in December 1924, Hemingway received a copy of a letter from George Doran to Donald Ogden Stewart
rejecting the *In Our Time* manuscript, with the suggestion that they
would be interested in publishing a novel first. Between then and the
last week of February 1925, Hemingway had no assurances that *In
Our Time* would fare any better with Boni and Liveright. Michael
Reynolds notes that during these two months in Schruns, Hemingway was in a dry spell, writing over thirty letters, but only the brief
fiction of "Banal Story." Thus, Hemingway had at least the motive
and the time to write this beginning; moreover, his mood was as
black as the first beard he was growing – like Emmett Hancock's –
and seems to have been directed at women who troubled the lives of
a number of his friends. Michael S. Reynolds, *Hemingway: The Paris
Years* (Oxford: Basil Blackwell, 1989).

29. Julian Smith, "Hemingway and the Thing Left Out," *Journal of Modern
Literature* 1 (1970): 169–72, reprinted in *The Short Stories of Ernest
Hemingway: Critical Essays*, ed. Jackson J. Benson (Durham, N.C.:
Duke University Press, 1975), pp. 135–47.

30. Audre Hanneman, *Ernest Hemingway: A Comprehensive Bibliography*
(Princeton, N.J.: Princeton University Press, 1969), pp. 182–3.

31. The passage is reprinted in Reynolds, *Hemingway's First War*, pp. 36–
7.

32. Reynolds, *Hemingway's First War*, chap. 6.

33. Recently revised by Earl Rovit and Gerry Brenner, *Ernest Hemingway*
(Boston: Twayne, 1986).

34. Arthur Waldhorn, *A Reader's Guide to Ernest Hemingway* (New York:
Farrar, Straus & Giroux, 1972), p. 69.

35. Colin S. Cass, "The Look of Hemingway's 'In Another Country',"
Studies in Short Fiction 18 (1981): 309–13. Brenner first argued that
Frederic Henry was telling the events soon after they occurred. James
Nagel's argument that Frederic told the tale some ten years later is in
"Catherine Berkley and Retrospection in *A Farewell to Arms*," *Ernest
Hemingway: Six Decades of Criticism*, ed. Linda W. Wagner (East Lan-
sing: Michigan State University Press, 1987); Brenner's rebuttal is in
American Literary Scholarship: An Annual/1987 (Durham, N. C.: Duke
University Press, 1989), pp. 157–8.

3

Distance, Voice, and Temporal Perspective in Frederic Henry's Narration: Successes, Problems, and Paradox

JAMES PHELAN

DESPITE the diverse, even contradictory, interpretations offered for *A Farewell to Arms* and its protagonist over the past
sixty years, Hemingway's handling of Frederic Henry's narration
has consistently been considered one of the novel's strengths.[1]
Whether critics argue that Frederic himself is self-pitying and pu-
sillanimous or self-sacrificing and tough, they typically credit
Hemingway with an impressive control of Frederic's narration, one
that allows the reader to build the appropriate inferences from
Frederic's tight-lipped descriptions. Yet I believe that precisely because the success of the narration is so often taken for granted, we
have not yet fully understood the communicative task that Hemingway set for himself, the means he chose to achieve it, and the
extent of his success. In assessing these matters here, I want to
examine, first, the techniques Hemingway uses to accomplish effectively the major part of his communicative task, second, a few
points in the novel where those techniques occasionally cannot
fully bear the burden placed upon them, and, finally, a striking
paradox in Frederic's narrative situation. My general purpose is to
see behind the famous Hemingway style to the intricacies of the
narration itself and to open up the subject of Hemingway's handling of the narration as a way of increasing our understanding of
Hemingway's achievement in *A Farewell to Arms*.

1

Let me begin with a brief overview of some terms and concepts
that I shall use in discussing the narration and with a brief sketch
of the way the narrative works as a whole. *Distance* will refer to the

53

relation between Hemingway as author and Frederic as narrator; it is a function of the extent to which Hemingway endorses Frederic's understanding of and judgments about the events he reports.[2] The distance between author and narrator may vary from one point in the narrative to another, but that relationship is always operating in our interpretation of a first-person narrator's statements. One way of judging distance is by attention to *voice*, a term that refers to the combination of style, tone, and values expressed in a discourse. When we detect a discrepancy between Hemingway's values and those expressed in Frederic's voice, we have the situation of a double-voiced discourse: Frederic's voice is contained within – and its communication is thereby complicated by – Hemingway's.[3] As someone telling his story in retrospect, Frederic can speak from his vantage point – or *vision* – at the *time of the action* or at the *time of the narration*.[4] Just as distance and voice may vary, so too may vision. *Self-consciousness* refers to Frederic's awareness of himself as the author of his autobiography, as the writer in control of the effects produced by his narrative. In analyzing these elements of the narration, I shall be concerned not just with describing them but also with understanding their consequences for the way Hemingway is shaping his whole narrative.

A Farewell to Arms recounts the growth of Frederic Henry: Initially a callow, unreflective youth who does not understand either the war in which he is involved or the woman who predicts to him that they will have a strange life together, he grows to a mature, strong man who understands the war, Catherine, the destructive world in which both have existed, and his own place in it. His movement from one state to the other is brought about through the interaction of his experiences in the war and his experiences with Catherine. The contrast between the war's destruction and Catherine's gentleness works on him until he comes to see what she has told him many times: The only thing one can be sure of in this world is that one will be destroyed. When he is faced with the deaths of their child and of Catherine herself, Frederic realizes the enormous value of what he has lost – yet he is not entirely defeated by this destruction. In the slow, careful walk he takes from the hospital to the hotel, he signifies his ability to go on living with dignity in spite of what he knows and has experienced; his walk signifies his potential to maintain some strength and honor in the face of the world's malevolence.

As we look at the narration at different stages of the novel, we shall complicate this understanding of the novel's movement. Let us begin with the novel's famous opening:

> In the late summer of that year we lived in a house in a village that looked across the river and the plain to the mountains. In the bed of the river there were pebbles and boulders, dry and white in the sun, and the water was clear and swiftly moving and blue in the channels. Troops went by the house and down the road and the dust they raised powdered the leaves of the trees. The trunks of the trees too were dusty and the leaves fell early that year and we saw the troops marching along the road and the dust rising and leaves, stirred by the breeze, falling and the soldiers marching and afterward the road bare and white except for the leaves. (p. 3)

This paragraph is often cited (and parodied) as a quintessential example of Hemingway's style, and in fact at least two critics have been moved to recast Frederic's prose into verse.[5] Perhaps because Frederic's style conforms so closely to our general notion of how Hemingway sounds, critics frequently do not inquire closely into the relations between author and narrator here. When we look closely, however, we can see that Hemingway is providing the ground for establishing a significant distance between himself and Frederic. The passage establishes a contrast between the natural landscape without the troops (the river is "clear and swiftly moving and blue") and that landscape with the troops ("the dust they raised powdered the leaves of the trees"), and it notes the disruption of nature's cycle by the troops ("and the leaves fell early that year"). Thus, despite the apparently objective description, the passage clearly conveys a negative judgment about the war.

It is less clear whether the source of the inference and the judgment is Hemingway or Frederic. Hemingway exploits the ambiguity of "and" to create the possibility that Frederic is telling us much more than he realizes – especially about himself. Hemingway is implying a causal relation between the presence of the troops and the falling of the leaves, but Frederic may not see that causation. As objective recorder, he may just be noting a sequence of events. We need to read further to settle this issue. Less ambiguously, the paragraph establishes Frederic as speaking from the time of the action: The past tense, which functions as narrative present, and the location of his perspective in space and time – at the window in the house in the village during the late summer and fall of "that year" – combine to orient us to his past rather than his current vision. Thus, the question whether or not Frederic sees the causal connection between the marching of the troops and the early falling of the leaves is the question whether or not his vision at the time of the narration includes an understanding of such causation.

As the chapter continues, we make further inferences about the negative incursions of the war into nature ("There were big guns too that passed in the day drawn by tractors, the long barrels of the guns covered with green branches and green leafy branches and vines laid over the tractors.") and a new inference about the association between rain and destruction:

> . . . in the fall when the rain came the leaves all fell from the chestnut trees and the branches were bare and the trunks black with rain. The vineyards were thin and bare-branched too and all the country wet and brown and dead with the autumn. . . .
>
> At the start of the winter came the permanent rain and with the rain came the cholera. But it was checked and in the end only seven thousand died of it in the army. (p. 4)

The last sentence resolves the ambiguity about the source of the inferences and judgments and thereby solidifies the distance between Frederic and Hemingway. Frederic the recorder, speaking from the time of the narration, does not detect the irony in the word "only." Instead, he is echoing another voice, one that can render the ravages of the cholera into a statistic about army casualties (the civilians are irrelevant to this voice) and that can dismiss the lives of seven thousand soldiers with the word "only." Frederic, in effect, is speaking with the voice of the military high command here, and Hemingway is double-voicing Frederic's speech. In this way, Hemingway is presenting Frederic not just as a naive narrator but also as a character who does not understand the war or the larger destruction of the world. Consequently, one of the generating features of the narrative is Frederic's inadequate view of his own situation; we read on in part to see the consequences of his faulty knowledge – and to see if his faulty vision will be corrected.

We shall return to the working of Frederic's early narration later, but for now I want to stress that despite the authority attached to Frederic's objective descriptions, Hemingway introduces him as someone whose values Hemingway questions rather than shares. I want to stress, too, that Hemingway's values are clearly (though, of course, not completely) announced in this chapter. The war is highly destructive; nature (in the rain-death-cholera link) can be as destructive. One measure of Frederic's distance from Hemingway will be where he stands in relation to this authorial norm.

Frederic's naiveté extends to his initial involvement with Catherine, but Hemingway's technique for revealing it is somewhat different. Frederic remains the objective recorder speaking from the time of the action, but one of the things he records is Catherine's dialogue. Be skillfully juxtaposing their conversations with Frederic's commentary, Hemingway again double-voices Frederic's narration. Here is Frederic's rendering of part of his third meeting with Catherine:

> "You did say you loved me, didn't you?"
> "Yes," I lied. "I love you." I had not said it before.
> "And you call me Catherine?"
> "Catherine." We walked on a way and were stopped under a tree.
> "Say, 'I've come back to Catherine in the night.' "
> "I've come back to Catherine in the night."
> "Oh, darling, you have come back, haven't you?"
> "Yes."
> "I love you so and it's been awful. You won't go away?" . . .
> . . . I kissed both her shut eyes. I thought she was probably a little crazy. It was all right if she was. I did not care what I was getting into. This was better than going every evening to the house for officers where the girls climbed all over you and put your cap on backward as a sign of affection between their trips upstairs with brother officers. I knew I did not love Catherine Barkley nor had any idea of loving her. This was a game, like bridge, in which you said things instead of playing cards. Like bridge you had to pretend you were playing for money or playing for some stakes. Nobody had mentioned what the stakes were. It was all right with me. . . .
> [Catherine:] "This is a rotten game we play, isn't it?"
> "What game?"
> "Don't be dull."
> "I'm not, on purpose."

"You're a nice boy," she said. "And you play it as well as you know how. But it's a rotten game."

"Do you always know what people think?"

"Not always. But I do with you. You don't have to pretend you love me. That's over for the evening." (pp. 30–1)

Clearly, Frederic's commentary is self-indicting in its selfishness, its calculation that playing this game with Catherine is better than going to the house for officers, its indifference to the consequences of his actions. But Hemingway's orchestration of the voices does more than that with the scene. Hemingway shows Catherine insisting that Frederic adopt a particular voice and speak the language of romantic love so that she, too, can adopt that voice. Yet to speak the language of love on command is to speak without sincerity, to mouth the words but be detached from the feelings they are intended to express. By thus commanding Frederic to speak a language that can never be sincerely spoken on command, Catherine puts herself in a position where her response to Frederic's words must also be at some remove from her feelings. To act as she does is indeed to act "a little crazy." Then, after Hemingway inserts Frederic's voice of selfishness in his address to the reader, the voice of the male on the make, Hemingway returns to Catherine and shows her speaking sincerely and frankly. The movement from her earlier voice to this one is so great that Frederic cannot keep up with it, and he tries to maintain the pretense of sincerity by feigning ignorance. With this move in the play among the voices, Hemingway shows us that Frederic's statement about what he is doing with Catherine is not only extremely selfish but also woefully inadequate in its understanding of Catherine and what she knows about the way each of them is behaving. Frederic is out of his depth with her, just as he is out of his depth in the war.

More generally, by establishing considerable distance from Frederic's commentary and some from Catherine's behavior in the earlier part of the scene, Hemingway is implicitly revealing his beliefs about love. It is unselfish, other-directed, based on honesty; Hemingway expresses some of what is implicit here in the priest's later words: "When you love you wish to do things for. You wish to sacrifice for. You wish to serve" (p. 72). Another significant measure of Frederic's distance from Hemingway will be where Frederic stands in relation to this authorial norm.

One of the striking features of *A Farewell to Arms* is how skillfully Hemingway gradually closes the distance between himself and Frederic and how he uses the narration to signal Frederic's changes. In Frederic's conversation with the priest after he returns from Milan to the front, Frederic articulates one of his traits, which in turn sheds light on Hemingway's general strategy in the novel: "I never think and yet when I begin to talk I say the things I have found out in my mind without thinking" (p. 179). Frederic typically recounts his experiences without commenting on his feelings and thoughts about them. The devices that Hemingway uses to have us assess Frederic's progress are, for the most part, the ones we have seen in the passages already discussed: asking us to see behind what Frederic explicitly says to what he unwittingly reveals; using the dialogue of another character to give us a perspective different from, and sometimes superior to, Frederic's. In addition, by making Frederic more of a recorder rather than a reflector, Hemingway is able to emphasize those places where Frederic does explicitly reveal his feelings. For example, when Frederic, after engaging in the drinking contest at the mess and then rushing to the hospital, only to find out that Catherine could not see him, tells us that "I had treated seeing Catherine very lightly, I had gotten somewhat drunk and had nearly forgotten to come but when I could not see her there I was feeling lonely and hollow" (p. 41), we see the passage as a very powerful signal of his movement past the attitudes expressed in the "I didn't care if she was crazy" passage. The importance of Frederic's feelings here is further emphasized by Hemingway's use of "there." The adverb indicates that Frederic's vision is shifting in this passage from the time of the action (when he says "to come," he is locating himself at the hospital) to the time of the narration (he steps back and looks at himself "there") and thereby indicates the importance of the event in Frederic's memory.

This passage, however, also illustrates Hemingway's habit of asking us to see more than Frederic tells us. Even as Frederic is moving past his "I don't care if she is crazy" attitude, he remains self-centered. He does not think about Catherine and how she might be feeling, though Ferguson has told him that Catherine is "not awfully well." He thinks only about himself and his feelings: "I felt lonely and hollow."

Hemingway combines all three features of his technique as he guides us to evaluate Frederic's claim that he loved Catherine during his summer of convalescence in Milan:

> Catherine Barkley was greatly liked by the nurses because she would do night duty indefinitely. She had quite a little work with the malaria people, the boy who had unscrewed the nose-cap was a friend of ours and never rang at night, unless it was necessary but between the times of working we were together. I loved her very much and she loved me. (p. 108)

Again Frederic seems to have advanced further in his regard for Catherine: He freely proclaims his love for her. But again we do not see much evidence of the love, other than his physical expression of it. It is Catherine who has "quite a little work" and who runs between his bed and "the times of working." Catherine gives; Frederic receives.

Soon after Frederic's summary of Catherine's nights, he records a conversation he had with Ferguson:

> "You ought to ask her not to do night duty for a while. She's getting very tired."
> "All right. I will."
> "I want to do it but she won't let me. The others are glad to let her have it. You might give her just a little rest."
> "All right." . . .
> "It would be better if you let her stay off nights a little while."
> "I want her to."
> "You do not. But if you would make her I'd respect you for it."
> "I'll make her."
> "I don't believe it." (p. 109)

Ferguson's remarks are telling not only because her voice is so authoritative and blunt (especially by contrast with Catherine, who would never contradict Frederic) but also because her remarks reinforce the inequality between Catherine and Frederic: Catherine does the giving; Frederic has the power. Catherine's going off night duty is all up to him – he has the capacity to "make" her do it. Again Frederic remains unaware of all that his faithful recording from his perspective at the time of the action reveals to us.

As Frederic's experiences accumulate, his narration alters in some subtle ways. The style remains the same, but the values expressed in the style – and thus Frederic's voice – change. This change in voice signals the closing of the distance between Frederic and Hemingway. Though Frederic's leap into the Tagliamento and away from the war is itself a spontaneous act of self-preservation, his narration of the retreat from Caporetto shows that he has been growing increasingly distant from the army and more concerned with returning to Catherine. He dreams of her and adopts her voice as he asks her if she would go away in the night.[6] While hiding in a barn during the retreat from Caporetto, Frederic's mind drifts away from the retreat to other times when he sat in a barn, and then he thinks: "You could not go back. If you did not go forward what happened? You never got back to Milan. And if you got back to Milan what happened?" He does not answer his question, but instead tells us "I listened to the firing to the north toward Udine" (p. 216). Although Frederic turns away from thinking about what will happen when he gets back to Milan, he now is demonstrating a commitment to Catherine that we have not seen before; furthermore, he is showing signs of reflecting on his behavior, moving from present to past to future in a way that we have not seen before. Given the way Hemingway has represented the destructiveness of the war and Catherine's commitment to Frederic, these signs of Frederic's changes are also signs of his movement toward Hemingway's values.

After his leap into the Tagliamento, Frederic comes to understand something of what Hemingway has been showing us about the destructiveness of the war. After his reunion with Catherine, Frederic moves very close to Hemingway's understanding of what it means to love. But the final steps of Frederic's movement toward Hemingway's values do not occur until the final pages of the narrative.[7] Frederic comes to know not just in the abstract but in actual experience how destructive the world can be. After he finds out that their child has died, he comments:

That was what you did. You died. You did not know what it was
about. . . . They threw you in and told you the rules and the first
time they caught you off base they killed you. Or they killed you
gratuitously like Aymo. Or gave you the syphilis like Rinaldi. But
they killed you in the end. (p. 327)

Both the emotion and the philosophical conclusions of the passage
give it a special emphasis. Frederic's view of the world now coin-
cides with Hemingway's, but their voices are not entirely in con-
cert: There is too much frustration and complaint in Frederic's
voice, qualities revealed most tellingly by the way the baseball
metaphor breaks down.

A short time later, however, after Frederic has experienced the
world's malevolence most painfully in Catherine's death, his voice
merges completely with Hemingway's. After learning of Catherine's death, after trying – and failing – to say a romantic good-bye
("it wasn't any good. It was like saying good-by to a statue"), he
reports his final action: "After a while I went out and left the
hospital and walked back to the hotel in the rain" (p. 332). Frederic has nothing else to learn; indeed, he has no reason even to
do anything else – "That was what you did. You died." But in
walking back out into the world, in going on with his life, and in
reporting his decision and his actions without complaint, Frederic
is also telling us how he is responding to his knowledge and his
experience. There is emotion in the reporting here, but it is emotion under control, the emotion of one who knows the painful
truth, who is suffering from the knowledge and experience of that
truth, but who is also moving beyond that knowledge and experience – not in the sense of forgetting it or discounting it but of
integrating it into an even larger view. It is a view that insists on
the possibility of going on with some measure of control and dignity despite the world's malevolence, despite even the strong re-
minder of that malevolence supplied by the rain. In giving Frederic
this last sentence, Hemingway is completing his portrait of Frederic's growth from unreflective and selfish youth to knowledge-
able and mature man. In giving him this last sentence, Hemingway
is also completing his own skillful handling of Frederic's unselfconscious record of his past.

2

We have seen that by making Frederic a character who is not much given to reflection on his experiences and by making him a narrator who is an unselfconscious but faithful recorder of those experiences, Hemingway has communicated more to us than Frederic is aware in two main ways: by asking us to see meanings in Frederic's accounts that Frederic himself is not aware of, and by using the dialogue of other characters to offer perspectives whose significance Frederic does not fathom. When might Frederic's traits as character and as narrator and Hemingway's techniques for communicating more than Frederic is aware meet some limits? In other words, are there times in the book when Hemingway's choices about how to handle Frederic's narration do not serve his purposes as well as he would like? With these questions in mind, I now want to consider two parts of the novel that seem to me to test the limits of what Hemingway can accomplish given Frederic's traits as narrator and character and given Hemingway's techniques for showing us more than Frederic is aware: Frederic's shooting the Italian sergeant and the representation of Catherine and Frederic's interlude in Switzerland.

As I briefly indicated earlier, one of Hemingway's tasks in his representation of the retreat from Caporetto is to trace Frederic's gradual evolution from a committed, competent leader in the ambulance corps to a justified fugitive who makes his separate peace. Early in the retreat, we see Frederic at his most decisive and most active: Leading Aymo, Bonello, and Piani, he decides that Aymo can bring the virgins, that they can give a ride to the sergeants, and that they should ride in a certain order, as well as when they should ride, when they should eat, when they should rest, and when they should get off the main road. In short, he is dedicated to carrying out their orders to get to Pordenone. He is also dedicated to certain values among the group: They share the food they find, they help each other out, they do not harm the girls, they help the sergeants, and they do not plunder the farmhouse where they stop for food. The sergeants, on the other hand, violate many of these values: They take the ride, but they want to save their own skins;

they enter the farmhouse to see what they can steal from it; having eaten themselves, they do not care whether or not the others eat. Their greatest violation occurs when the ambulance gets stuck and they take off. All this, I think, comes through Frederic's narration very clearly. The problems arise when Frederic reacts to their most egregious offense – their abandoning the others when the ambulance gets stuck – by shooting at them and wounding one, who is then killed, with Frederic's approval, by Bonello.

How much distance is there between Hemingway and Frederic at this point? Does Hemingway want us to see Frederic's response as justified in some way? Or is the shooting a sign that the violence of the war is infecting Frederic as well? What is the significance of the placement of the incident so soon after Frederic's dream about being together with Catherine again? How does the incident fit in with the two other shootings during the retreat – Aymo's by the Germans, and those by the carabinieri at the Tagliamento? Developing satisfactory answers to these questions is, I think, an extremely murky business – in large part because of the first-person perspective.

Just as we can be confident that Hemingway does not endorse the values behind the assertion at the end of the first chapter, we can be confident that he does not fully endorse Frederic's reaction here. Given Hemingway's attitudes about the war's destruction, we can infer that shooting to kill under these circumstances is clearly overdoing it. One sign of Hemingway's disapproval is that he slightly distances Frederic from the killing by having Bonello fire the fatal shot. If Hemingway wholeheartedly endorsed the shooting, it would make sense to have one of Frederic's shots kill the man. Bonello's dialogue also provides a clue to Hemingway's values here: Bonello is proud of what he has done, but his boasting reveals the problems with his viewpoint – ". . . all my life I've wanted to kill a sergeant" (p. 207). His joke about what he will say in confession, "Bless me, father, I killed a sergeant," also underscores this reading of Frederic's action. When we recall the standard way of beginning a confession, "Bless me, father, for I have sinned," we can see how Hemingway is double-voicing Bonello's utterance here. Bonello is not just melding the language of war onto the language of religion; he is also transforming the confession of guilt into a source of pride

– bless me, for I did something good in killing the sergeant. By asking us to read the religious formula underneath Bonello's line, Hemingway reminds us that Bonello has in one sense "sinned." Significantly, Bonello's joke does not succeed with Frederic; he reports not that "we all laughed" but that "they all laughed" (p. 208). Frederic's inability – or unwillingness – to laugh is a further sign that he has overreacted. Although Frederic never reflects on the incident, we see that one source of his uneasiness is that he has been operating by the same code of war that sanctions Bonello's actions and Bonello's comments. The code says that a commanding officer has the right to command obedience; violations of that command are punishable by death. Despite other moves Frederic has been making away from the war, he is still very bound by the military mentality.

But Hemingway, I think, wants to communicate other things with the scene as well. His representation of the sergeants as consistently violating the values of sharing and respect by which Frederic and the others are living suggests that the scene is also showing Frederic taking some kind of stand about those values. This issue is important, because Frederic earlier had been someone who simply did what was easiest. By showing Frederic reacting so strongly to the sergeants' violations of the group's values, Hemingway is showing – or trying to show – some significant change in Frederic as well. Again, Hemingway's technique for conveying this aspect of the incident is the use of another character's dialogue. Immediately after the shooting, Piani delivers a judgment about the sergeants whose accuracy we must recognize: "the dirty scum" (p. 204). Then later he returns the group's conversation to Frederic's action, saying with approval, "You certainly shot that sergeant, Tenente" (p. 207).

Viewed in this way, the incident becomes an important checkpoint by which to measure the alterations Frederic undergoes during the retreat. When he shoots the sergeant, he is simultaneously entrapped in the code of the military and committed to values that will eventually move him to make his separate peace. The subsequent events of the retreat, especially the shooting of Aymo and the executions at the Tagliamento, push him finally and completely away from the military code.

The trouble with this view of the incident is that I am not sure it is fully substantiated by the narration. The reading hangs heavily on the few lines of dialogue given to Bonello and Piani – and even more on my sense of how what Hemingway is doing with Frederic in the rest of the novel has implications for what he needs to do with his character here. The dialogue of the minor characters, especially Piani's, seems susceptible to alternate interpretations: Piani can be seen as closer to Bonello than my reading suggests; Piani does, after all, laugh at Bonello's joke. The more positive side of Frederic's action may not really be built into the incident. But then Hemingway's previous choices in representing the sergeants and in showing Frederic's commitment to certain values seem problematical. This second-guessing of my reading is not meant to dislodge it, but only to indicate that I do not believe that it can be as well substantiated as the earlier interpretations I have offered. The larger point is that if Hemingway had given Frederic different traits as a narrator and a character, if Frederic not only recorded but explicitly interpreted the incident through reflecting on it, Hemingway would be able to communicate its complexities far more firmly than he can through Frederic's tight-lipped, recording, time-of-the-action perspective. But to alter Frederic that way would be to lose much of the power of the rest of the book.

The situation with the events in Switzerland is both similar and different. Hemingway again, I think, wants to accomplish something complex: to show that Frederic and Catherine have reached a place that is both idyllic and impossible to maintain; to show also that Frederic and Catherine sense that their life has no future; to show further that if the world were different, Catherine and Frederic would always be very happy, and that the reason they are only sometimes happy lies not with them but with that world and their knowledge of it. All these effects will serve the larger purposes of his narrative: By showing that their union is very attractive, he will increase the sense of loss we feel in Catherine's death. By showing that they have no real future, he will reinforce his thematic point about the malevolence of the world. By showing that they sense their own plight, he will add another dimension to their situation and will be able to make a further thematic point about how best to respond to a knowledge of the world.[8]

Part of Hemingway's strategy in Chapters XXXVIII to XL is to use Frederic's narration to achieve these different effects at different times, but there are places where the effects interact with each other. Consider the end of Chapter XXXVIII. Frederic reports that he and Catherine awaken in the night. She had been thinking, she says, about the time when they first met and she was a "little crazy"; she insists that she is now no longer crazy, just "very, very, very happy" (p. 300), and she proposes that they both go back to sleep at exactly the same moment. The disturbance underneath her waking and her proclamation of happiness prevents Frederic from going back to sleep when she does. "I was awake for quite a long time thinking about things and watching Catherine sleeping, the moonlight on her face" (p. 301).

Why should Catherine wake? Because she, who has known about the world all along, knows that their idyll cannot last, and she is disturbed by that knowledge. Why should Frederic not be able to fall back asleep? Because he senses what she knows. He makes a similar point at the end of Chapter XL: "We knew the baby was very close now and it gave us both a feeling as though something were hurrying us and we could not lose any time together" (p. 311). But earlier in Chapter XXXVIII, Hemingway has also used Frederic's record of a long conversation with Catherine to show that she is worried about his feelings for her, a worry that also comes from her recognition that they have no real future. In the conversation, Catherine asks Frederic if he is bored or restless; she asks him about his having gonorrhea and says that she wishes she had had it, that she wants to be exactly like him. Hemingway's sexism comes through clearly here, but so does a rather different consequence of Catherine's worry about their future. Her fear of what is coming also makes her somewhat desperate about the present: There seems to be some lack in the here and now that she wants to fill. Thus, when she wakes at night and proclaims that she is very, very, very happy, we cannot help inferring that she protests too much.

But how do I know that it is her fear of the future that makes her desperate about the present? One could plausibly argue that her desperation is a sign of Frederic's current inadequacy and her own endless insecurity. Again, I think that what has happened is that

Hemingway has run up against the limitations of his narrative perspective, only here those limitations become even stronger because of the sexism. Just as Hemingway turns in the shooting incident from Frederic's recording to the dialogue of Piani and Bonello to create his effects, he turns here to Catherine's dialogue. In addition to the limits Hemingway faces as a consequence of Frederic's tight-lipped recording, he faces the problem of the way the narrative perspective constrains our view of Catherine. Because the perspective allows us to see Catherine only from outside – and because Hemingway has conceived her character in such a sexist way – her conversation can give rise to the interpretation that the trouble with their life in Switzerland is not the world but the two of them. Such an interpretation alters our view of Catherine's death: It becomes not the culmination of the tragedy but a convenient way for Frederic to escape from this sterile, constricted relationship. Although I think that the larger progression of the narrative finally calls such an interpretation into question, I want to emphasize that in this case the consequences of the limits of the first-person narrative perspective may be very significant indeed.

I turn finally to the way in which much of what I have been saying about Frederic's narration implies that it is built on a paradox. Strikingly, this paradox has the potential to undermine the novel's illusion of realism; yet that potential is never realized. The paradox arises from three features of the narration, two of which have already been discussed explicitly: (1) With few exceptions, Frederic speaks from his perspective at the time of the action. (2) A related point: Any growth or change in Frederic's character occurs at the time of the action, not during the time of the narration or through the act of narration. Thus, when I read the last sentence of the novel ("After a while I went out and left the hospital and walked back to the hotel in the rain.") as a sign of Frederic's growth, I am also understanding that the growth occurred then. The understated style is capturing Frederic's control during his walk, not a control that he has acquired through the act of writing. (3) Frederic is a recorder, not a self-conscious narrator. He is intent on telling his story, but he is no artist, no Humbert Humbert trying to render the most artistically effective narrative that he can muster in order to give immortality to his beloved.

68

Because it is always possible – even easy – to find confirmation for the hypothesis that Frederic is self-consciously crafting the narrative (it is clearly his story, and his story clearly shows evidence of careful crafting), this last point may need further demonstration. The view of Frederic as recorder is, I think, superior to the view of Frederic as self-conscious narrator on two grounds. First, one of the conventions of first-person narration is that we take the narrator as non-self-conscious unless we are given reason to do otherwise; non-self-conscious first-person narration is the unmarked case. Thus, when we encounter a first-person narrator, we assume that the narrator is not the source of such things as foreshadowing, patterns of imagery, parallelism of incidents, the lyricism of a particular style – unless we have some signal that calls our attention to the narrator's self-consciousness. For example, when Huck Finn describes the sunrise over the Mississippi in sentences with impressive poetic power, we do not marvel at his artistic prowess and his selective display of it; instead, we see Huck as the window through which Twain's artistry is being revealed. On the other hand, when Nabokov wants to create Humbert Humbert as a self-conscious narrator, he has Humbert frequently comment on his own narration: In chapter one, he says that, "you can always count on a murderer for a fancy prose style." Later, he laments: "Oh my Lolita, I have only words to play with!" Finally, of course, he talks about his narrative – and its artistry – as an attempt to compensate for the crimes he has committed against Lolita: "I see nothing for the treatment of my misery but the melancholy and very local palliative of articulate art." "One had to choose between [Clare Quilty] and H. H., and one wanted H. H. to exist at least a couple of months longer so as to have him make you live in the minds of later generations. I am thinking of aurochs and angels, the secret of durable pigments, prophetic sonnets, the refuge of art." Frederic is clearly more like Huck than like Humbert.

The second reason that I want to argue for Frederic as recorder is the internal evidence of the narration. An especially telling example occurs in Chapter VII just before Frederic proclaims that the war "seemed no more dangerous to me myself than war in the movies" (p. 37). Frederic mentions that he had met two British gunners when he was on leave in Milan. "They were big and shy and embarrassed and very appreciative together of anything that happened. I *wish* that I was with the British. It would have been much simpler. Still I would probably have been killed. Not in this ambulance business. Yes, even in the ambulance business. British ambulance drivers were killed sometimes. Well, I knew I would not be killed" (emphasis added). The passage indicates Frederic's habit as a recorder: His reactions here arise out of the stream of his recollections, rather than being motivated by his conscious artistic purpose. When he thinks of the British gunners at the time of narration, he jumps to his wish of having been with them because it would have been much simpler. But then he catches himself up by thinking of the possible negative consequences of that situation; then he has a short dialogue with himself about whether or not he would have been killed; then he quickly ends that by giving his view that the war is not real to him. To say that Frederic has planned all these shifts for some artistic purpose of his own is to make an interpretive leap for which the narration provides no spring.

The paradoxical consequence of these three features of the narration can be effectively illustrated by returning to my reading of the sentences ending the first chapter: "At the start of the winter came the permanent rain and with the rain came the cholera. But it was checked and in the end only seven thousand died of it in the army." The rub in seeing Frederic as the victim rather than the source of the irony is that if non-self-conscious Frederic has in fact learned about the war and the world at the time of the action, then this knowledge should always be a part of his perspective as he retells the story. In other words, Frederic writes as if he does not know what he in fact knows – and he is not deliberately suppressing his knowledge or manipulating our understanding of his knowledge for any conscious artistic purpose of his own. In short, the narrative situation does not make mimetic sense.

Yet this paradoxical situation of Frederic's narration does not destroy the mimetic illusion of the narrative. Why? First, because the narration makes artistic sense, and second, because it makes sense in such a way that there is no reason for the reader to register the paradox during the actual temporal experience of the narrative. Hemingway, in effect, wants to write a *Bildungsroman* with a tragic twist. If he were to do that from a third-person perspective, there would be no problem in showing that the protagonist started out in ignorance and ended in knowledge. The narrator and the audience would start out ahead of the character, but eventually he would catch up to and perhaps surpass the audience. But to tell such a story from the perspective of a protagonist who would unselfconsciously record his experiences and some of his judgments and beliefs at the time of the action would have some significant advantages. Such a narration would allow the audience to have a deeper, more intimate relation with that protagonist, and such a relation might be necessary for the audience to maintain partial sympathy for him in the early stages of the narrative. Such a narration would also necessarily involve the audience in a great deal of inferential activity that would in itself be a source of the narrative's pleasure. Furthermore, although this procedure would entail the paradoxical situation described earlier, it would not be noticed. It would not be noticed because as one reads the early chapters – and, indeed, the middle and later chapters – one does not know whether or not the narrator will attain any more knowledge than he has at the time of the narration. Thus, when we read the last sentence of Chapter I in the temporal progression of the novel, we are not aware of the paradox, because we do not know that Frederic comes to an understanding of the war and the world that would make it impossible for him to utter such a sentence without being ironic.

If the analysis in this essay has been at all persuasive, then I think it suggests several noteworthy conclusions about Frederic's narration. First, it indicates the subtlety and skill with which Hemingway handles that narration. Second, in showing that the technique has limits as well as powers, it offers an account for some of the interpretive disagreement about the novel that accuses neither Hemingway nor his critics of being butchers. The disagreements stem not from sloppiness but from divergent inferences that naturally arise as Hemingway bumps up against the limits of his technique. Third, in showing that according to the standards of naturalistic probability Frederic could not logically tell his story as he does, the analysis suggests something about the conventions of first-person narration. We shall overlook the mimetic impossibility in order to allow Hemingway to tell the story in the most effective way – provided that the awareness of the impossibility is not foregrounded by the narrative itself. Taken together, these conclusions point to the complexity of the narration in *A Farewell to Arms* and suggest that the full depth of that complexity is yet to be plumbed.

NOTES

1. For a sampling of divergent opinions, see Gerry Brenner, *Concealments in Hemingway's Fiction* (Columbus: Ohio State University Press, 1983), Scott Donaldson, *By Force of Will: The Life and Art of Ernest Hemingway* (New York: Viking Press, 1977), Earl Rovit, *Ernest Hemingway*, 2nd ed. (Boston: Twayne, 1985), Philip Young, *Ernest Hemingway: A Reconsideration* (New York: Harcourt, Brace, 1966), Carlos Baker, *Hemingway: The Writer as Artist*, 3rd ed. (Princeton, N.J.: Princeton University Press, 1963), Robert Lewis, *Hemingway on Love* (Austin: University of Texas Press, 1965). For sharp criticisms, see Judith Fetterley, *The Resisting Reader: A Feminist Approach to American Fiction* (Bloomington: Indiana University Press, 1978), and Millicent Bell, "*A Farewell to Arms:* Pseudoautobiography and Personal Metaphor," in *Ernest Hemingway: The Writer in Context*, ed. James Nagel (Madison: University of Wisconsin Press, 1984).

   For a sampling of treatments of Hemingway's technique in the novel, see Michael Reynolds, *Hemingway's First War: The Making of ''A Farewell to Arms''* (Princeton, N.J.: Princeton University Press, 1976), Daniel Schneider, "Hemingway's *A Farewell to Arms:* The Novel as Pure Poetry," in *Ernest Hemingway: Five Decades of Criticism*, ed. Linda W. Wagner (East Lansing: Michigan State University Press, 1974), pp. 252–66, Larzer Ziff, "The Social Basis of Hemingway's Style," in *Ernest Hemingway: Six Decades of Criticism*, ed. Linda W. Wagner (East Lansing: Michigan State University Press, 1987), pp. 147–54, James Phelan, *Reading People, Reading Plots: Character, Progression, and the Interpretation of Narrative* (University of Chicago Press, 1989), and James Phelan, *The Concept of Voice, the Voices of Frederic Henry, and the Structure of A Farewell to Arms* (Oxford University Press, 1990). Some of the material in the early part of this essay is adapted from these previous analyses.
2. For further discussion, see Wayne C. Booth, *The Rhetoric of Fiction*, 2nd ed. (University of Chicago Press, 1983), especially the chapter entitled "The Control of Distance in *Emma*."

3. For further discussion, see Mikhail Bakhtin, "Discourse in the Novel," in *The Dialogic Imagination,* trans. Caryl Emerson (Austin: University of Texas Press, 1981), and Phelan, "The Concept of Voice."

4. For further discussion, see Gérard Genette, *Narrative Discourse: An Essay in Method,* trans. Jane Lewin (Ithaca, N.Y.: Cornell University Press, 1982).

5. Reynolds, *Hemingway's First War,* p. 56, and Bernard Oldsey, *Hemingway's Hidden Craft: The Writing of "A Farewell to Arms"* (University Park: Pennsylvania State University Press, 1979), p. 64.

6. For more on this passage, see Phelan, "The Concept of Voice."

7. Frederic actually articulates Hemingway's beliefs about the world in Chapter XXXV in the famous "if people bring so much courage to this world" passage, but because that passage is spoken from the time of the narration, it comes before we see how Frederic arrives at the knowledge. One consequence of the placement of the passage is that as we read it, we regard Frederic less as character and more as mouthpiece for Hemingway; a second consequence is that we shift our narrative interest from whether or not the distance between Frederic and Hemingway will close to how.

8. For some differing views on Frederic and Catherine's relationship, especially as it is represented in Chapters XXXVIII to XL, see the works by Robert Lewis, Judith Fetterley, and Millicent Bell cited in note 1.

4

Hemingway's Unknown Soldier: Catherine Barkley, the Critics, and the Great War

SANDRA WHIPPLE SPANIER

PERHAPS no character in all of Hemingway's fiction has provoked responses so numerous, so contradictory, and so strong as has Catherine Barkley of *A Farewell to Arms*. She has been idealized and reviled; her creator has been reviled for idealizing her. She has been called a "passionate priestess," a "divine lollipop," the "pulse of the transcendent," an "inflated rubber-doll woman."[1] Some readers have objected to her passivity; others have found her malevolently active. Yet for nearly half a century a single, virtually unquestioned premise has provided the basis for these wildly divergent views: that there are two types of Hemingway women, those who destroy men and those whom men could only dream of. And Catherine Barkley long has been accepted as the prototypical dream girl, the classic "amoeba-like" Hemingway heroine.[2]

Of Hemingway's protagonists in general, Michael Reynolds has astutely observed that "the critical patterns have been so inhibiting that the individual characters have almost been lost. Approaching a Hemingway novel today is like restoring a Renaissance painting that has been clouded by several layers of varnish."[3] My purpose in this essay is to reexamine the ways in which the layers of critical opinion over the past sixty years may have colored or clouded our view of *A Farewell to Arms* and to reframe in its original historical and cultural context Hemingway's ironic tragedy of the Great War. I do so in the hope of restoring the portrait of his complex and underestimated heroine, Catherine Barkley.

The earliest reviewers of the novel remarked its "complete contemporaneity" and considered Hemingway a spokesman for his generation.[4] One critic, writing for the *New York Times Book Review* of September 29, 1929, declared that the "real story" – the love story – "could only have come in the war and out of the war."[5] In succeeding decades, however, too many critics in dealing with Catherine Barkley have all but forgotten that she is functioning in the environment of a brutal and irrational war – a war that, by extension, becomes a metaphor for the conditions of life itself in our time. Yet it is in this original context that Catherine emerges in her full outline as the truly heroic figure of the novel. As much a victim of the war as her fiancé who was killed, Catherine has made a deliberate retreat into a private world of her own construction, within the perimeter of which she can achieve at least a limited autonomy.[6] Her willingness to submerge herself in a personal relationship, far from being a sign of female spinelessness, is an act of will. A model of courage and stoic self-awareness, Catherine is determined to forge a meaningful and orderly existence – if only temporarily – in a world in which all traditional notions of meaning and order have been shattered. Jake Barnes, another casualty of the Great War, declared in *The Sun Also Rises*, "I did not care what it was all about. All I wanted to know was how to live in it."[7] Catherine Barkley is one of the "initiated." She has a fair idea of what it is all about, and it is her part to teach Frederic by example how to live in it.

Catherine Barkley and the Critics

To begin, a brief survey of the prevailing critical views of Catherine Barkley is in order. Edmund Wilson's observation in 1939 of a "split attitude" and "growing antagonism" toward women in Hemingway's work provided a basic premise of Hemingway criticism for decades to come. He saw Hemingway's heroines as falling into two categories: the "submissive infra-Anglo-Saxon women that make his heroes such perfect mistresses" and "American bitches of the most soul-destroying sort." Suspecting that Hemingway's "instinct to get the woman down" grows out of "a fear that the woman will get the man down," Wilson was the first to suggest that Catherine is a victim of Hemingway's hostility toward women: "Even the hero of *A Farewell to Arms* eventually destroys

Catherine — after enjoying her abject devotion — by giving her a baby, itself born dead." Another truism was born when Wilson declared that Hemingway "has not shown any very solid sense of character, or indeed, any real interest in it," that Frederic and Catherine are not "convincing as human personalities." Rather, "we find merely an idealized relationship, the abstractions of a lyric emotion."[8] In the first study to focus exclusively on Hemingway's women, published in 1950, we find that Theodore Bardacke has absorbed Wilson's assumptions and taken a position regarding Catherine that will prove typical. Declaring that her "complete subjection is the core of Hemingway's conception of the ideal woman," Bardacke concludes that "Catherine, for all her womanliness, was the ruin of Lieutenant Henry through her isolating love."[9]

The founding fathers of Hemingway scholarship, Philip Young and Carlos Baker, each of whom published a ground-breaking book in 1952, also accept the notion of Catherine's idealization, but they view her positively. "Idealized beyond the fondest wishes of most people, and even the more realistic wishes of some," Catherine is "both the first true 'Hemingway heroine' and the most convincing one," says Young.[10] Baker takes Edmund Wilson to task for disparaging Hemingway's female characters on the grounds that they are unrealistic and embody only two extremes ("This fact is taken to be a kind of sin of omission."); he counters that "the whole movement of the novel is from concretion toward abstraction." He finds the book "essentially poetic in its conception and execution" and sees Catherine as the embodiment of one of the two conceptual poles of the novel: the "Home concept," as opposed to all that is "Not-Home."[11]

Other critics sympathetic to Catherine have seen her as a kind of affirmative force, the embodiment of the female principle. She is the "anima-mother" who aids in Frederic's moral growth as he learns to bid "farewell to a not-caringness," a "passionate priestess" ministering to Frederic's needs, the archetypal feminine through whom Frederic, the "embattled masculine," can feel "the pulse of the transcendent," the representation of "female faith" opposing in an "unresolved 'dialectic'" Frederic's "male skepticism."[12] Capable of sacrifice and selfless love, she has been seen as more noble than Frederic, whom Scott Donaldson terms a "selfish lover," unworthy of her.[13]

Yet to others, the "dream girl" is a nightmare. A number of male critics see Catherine as a destructive force, all the more deadly in her sweet disguise, and they view her death as a blessing. Leo Gurko finds her "so terrifyingly and clingingly in love" with Frederic that she becomes his "leechlike shadow."[14] According to Richard Hovey, "such a disvaluing by Catherine of her own self, such a need to flee the normal burdens of selfhood, indicates that her love is feverish in its dependency," and he concludes that "however lyrical is the affair in this novel, the love impulses in it are fettered by sadism and death wishes."[15] Preferring agape to eros, Robert Lewis sees in Catherine "Circe-like powers to ruin her lover" by keeping him "mired in the contradictions and follies of 'true love'." Her death carries "the hope with it of the destruction of her destructive love that excludes the world."[16] J. F. Kobler, in an article with the rather hostile title "Let's Run Catherine Barkley Up the Flagpole and See Who Salutes," scorns not only Hemingway's "bedridden lovers" but all who believe in the "hopeless romantic love" that she represents, namely, "practically every undergraduate female – those emotionally so registered as well as those academically enrolled."[17]

Equally negative about Catherine Barkley, some female critics likewise find malevolent forces at work in the novel – not in the form of the pitiful creation that they regard as "passive femininity incarnate" but in Hemingway's "acute fear of female domination."[18] While again traceable back to Wilson, this view was more firmly reinforced by Leslie Fiedler, who claims that "had Catherine lived, she could only have turned into a bitch; for this is the fate in Hemingway's imagination of all Anglo-Saxon women."[19] Interestingly, the feminists who follow this tack assume the same premises as the most chauvinist of male critics who are glad to see Catherine dead: that, as Katharine Rogers asserts in her study of misogyny in literature, his ideal women "resemble more the creations of erotic fantasy than real people; his realistically depicted women are generally engaged in destroying the men around them."[20] Joyce Carol Oates, basing her judgment partially on reports of the biographical Hemingway's alleged dislike of women "who did not know their place vis-á-vis men," declares that "since he rarely wrote of women with sympathy, and virtually never with subtlety and understanding, feminist charges of misogyny are surely justified."[21] In the most concentrated attack, Judith Fetterley maintains that "Catherine's contradictions are *not* resolvable because her character is determined by forces outside of her; it is a reflection of male psychology and male fantasy life and is understandable only when seen as a series of responses to the male world that surrounds her." She calls the novel Hemingway's "resentful cryptogram" of fear and hostility toward women, in which the female's threat to male freedom must be killed off – the point of Catherine's death is that "the only good woman is a dead one, and even then there are questions."[22]

Finally, a growing number of critics are realizing a depth and complexity in some of Hemingway's female characters long obscured, perhaps, by the critical commonplaces and by the public persona of the author himself.[23] These views, multiplying rapidly in the 1980s, are not without precedent in Hemingway studies. In 1963, Alan Holder argued that Hemingway's attitudes toward his women characters were more complex than had been generally recognized, although he did not discuss Catherine.[24] In 1980, Linda Wagner reminded us that, at least in Hemingway's early fiction, "the women have already reached that plateau of semi-stoic self-awareness which Hemingway's men have, usually, yet to attain," but she felt that Catherine's "submissiveness and languor" disqualified her from that company.[25] Yet a few critics *have* seen Catherine's strength and recognized her crucial role in the education of Frederic Henry. As early as 1949, Ray B. West, Jr., noted that it takes Catherine's death to teach Frederic what she had known from the beginning: that death is "the end of it." Jackson Benson, writing two decades later, admired Catherine's bravery and acknowledged "how prominent a place in his consciousness and value system Catherine and the meaning structure called 'home' has achieved." In the mid-1970s, Robert Merrill remarked that few have recognized Catherine as Frederic's equal as an *initiate* who knows the tragic nature of the world.[26] Delbert Wylder and Michael Reynolds call her the hero of the novel.[27] But however sympathetic these critics have been toward Catherine, the matter of her character has not been the main concern of their discussions. Rather, her role as hero or initiate most often has simply been suggested in passing – relegated to a sentence or two in the context of other arguments. Judith Wexler's 1981 article "E.R.A. for Hemingway: A Feminist Defense of *A Farewell to Arms*" was the first sustained argument for Catherine's overlooked strength of character.[28] My own view falls within this critical camp, although I give Catherine even more credit as the exemplary figure of the novel than would most of my predecessors. I read Catherine Barkley not simply as a strong and sympathetic character, but as the one character in the novel who, more than any other, embodies the controls of courage and honor that many have called the "Hemingway code." As one who knows the world and has devised as best she can a way to live in it, she serves as a mentor to Frederic Henry.

Reading the character of Catherine Barkley is, indeed, "dizzying in its complexity and contradictions," as James Phelan has observed.[29] Given such a wide array of readings of Catherine Barkley, some mutually exclusive, how is one to evaluate the validity of any particular view? In his penetrating analysis of Judith Fetterley's "resistant" feminist reading, Phelan poses the issue this way:

> Since any one character, incident, or narrative comment can easily be recontextualized and offered in support of countless covert messages (one could, for example, construct a hypothesis about Hemingway's covert negative message about Switzerland on the basis of Catherine's dying there or a positive one on the basis of its being like the priest's homeland, the Abruzzi), the plausibility of any one hypothesis will depend in large part on its being anchored in a recognizable pattern in the overt story.

He goes on to argue that "the understanding of that pattern and its effects . . . must be confirmed or disconfirmed by the understanding of the whole." In other words, Catherine's character must be considered in terms of the overall movement of the novel.

Here, according to Phelan, is where Fetterley's case breaks down: "If the only significant progression is the gradual revelation of the hostility of men to women, then the covert message of Catherine's death would be that she died because she was a woman. If, however, her assumption about the progression does not hold up, then much of her case will be in jeopardy, because in effect the narrative that she is resisting will not be Hemingway's." But the "progression" of the novel concerns a matter far larger than any revelation of Hemingway's sexism. Rather, it concerns "Frederic's slow evolution into a mature man who both learns and faces up to what the narrative presents as the overwhelming truth of his existence." Catherine plays a vital role in bringing about that developing awareness.

The same kind of case that Phelan makes to refute Fetterley's argument might be made against any number of other critical readings of Catherine Barkley that do not take into account her function in relation to the novel's theme. For example, if Catherine is read as a passive–aggressive siren whose death liberates Frederic from her isolating romantic love, then is the entire point of Hemingway's novel that women are dangerous, or that men must not be distracted from their responsibilities in the social world? While such readings conceivably might apply to other of Hemingway's works, they distort or disregard the tragic and ironic impact of *A Farewell to Arms*. The manner of Catherine's life and death is an inextricable element of the novel's design and vital to a central theme: that the world breaks everyone, and there can be no lasting "separate peace."[30]

Catherine Barkley and the Great War

In restoring the portrait of Catherine Barkley, it is crucial that we keep firmly in mind not only the thematic aspects of *A Farewell to Arms* but also its cultural and historical context. Edmund Wilson, writing in 1939, was able to see the timeliness of Hemingway's work:

> Going back over Hemingway's books today, we can see clearly what an error of the politicos it was to accuse him of an indifference to society. His whole work is a criticism of society: he has responded to every pressure of the moral atmosphere of the time, as it is felt at the roots of human relations, with a sensitivity almost unrivaled.[31]

Wilson called him a "gauge of morale."

In 1926, C. G. Jung had a troubling dream of being shelled from the "other side" and interpreted it as a suggestion that "the war, which in the outer world had taken place some years before, was not yet over, but was continuing to be fought with the psyche."[32] Hemingway spent nearly the entire decade following the war writing about it. Malcolm Cowley, in his 1932 review of *Death in the Afternoon*, observed that "the War, to judge from his books, has been the central experience in his career; he shows the effects of it more completely than any other American novelist."[33] Philip Young, in his classic study, argues that Hemingway's own wounding in World War I made a profound and lasting impact on his fiction. Mark Spilka takes the position that whereas Frederic Henry's disillusion with the war occurs on the retreat from Caporetto, "Ernest's was a postwar acquisition – much of it inspired by literary sources":

> He had absorbed his antiwar sentiments from postwar readings of poets like Owen and Sassoon and novelists like Ford and Dos Passos. What he had read squared, however, with the military histories which then absorbed him, and with what he had personally heard and seen at and behind the front; and it squared also with the disillusionment of his postwar return to Oak Park, where his own war stories had gradually palled and gone out of fashion.[34]

That Hemingway was a voracious reader and that his reading helped to shape his fiction is well documented.[35] (Gertrude Stein said that "he looks like a modern and he smells of museums."[36]) But whether experience or collective memory, the source of Hemingway's postwar-generation sensibilities is beside the point here.

As Paul Fussell has demonstrated in his valuable study *The Great War and Modern Memory*, World War I profoundly determined many of the prevailing myths of our century, especially as reflected in the writing of the twenties and thirties.[37] *A Farewell to Arms* is in many ways paradigmatic of the fiction of the Great War. The principal problem with most of the interpretations of Catherine Barkley's character, as Roger Whitlow has pointed out, is that most critics have judged her actions and speeches against "normal" behavior.[38] The world in which she and Frederic live is far from normal. When we consider *A Farewell to Arms* as a novel of the

Great War by a young writer considered at the time a spokesman for the generation that Malcolm Cowley declared in 1929 still "undemobilized,"[39] the view of Catherine as initiate and exemplar becomes far clearer.

It must be remembered that World War I was a mechanized horror unprecedented in human history, a war of "stasis and futility" that exacted casualties hideous in their nature and number – and for no reason that anyone could understand. After great engagements like Verdun had proved nothing except that a million men could die in a single battle without changing so much as the front line, even Ambassador Walter Hines Page, whose views were typical of the Anglophile and prowar enthusiasts in the United States, "could despair of 'a crazy world – a slaughterhouse where madness dwells.'"[40] Two and a half decades later, Hemingway himself called World War I "the most colossal, murderous, mismanaged butchery that has ever taken place on earth" and commented that "the worst generals it would be possible to develop by a process of reverse selection of brains carried on over a thousand years could never make a worse mess than Passchendaele and Gallipoli."[41]

Indeed, in discussing Hemingway's world view as expressed in his fiction, several critics, without referring to the Great War specifically, describe its mental landscape precisely. "It is a world seen through a crack in a wall by a man who is pinned down by gunfire," says Philip Young:

> Hemingway's world is one in which things do not grow and bear fruit, but explode, break, decompose, or are eaten away. . . . It is a barren world of fragments which lies before us like a land of bad dreams, where a few pathetic idylls and partial triumphs relieve the diet of nightmare. It has neither light nor love that lasts nor certitude nor peace nor much help for pain. It is swept with the actualities of struggle and flight, and up ahead in the darkness the armies are engaged.[42]

It is, in Robert Penn Warren's words, "a terrain for which the maps have been mislaid."[43]

Catherine's fiancé was killed in the battle of the Somme, the British attack that began on July 1, 1916, and cost them 60,000 casualties on that day alone without gaining any ground whatever.[44] The fighting continued for four months until stopped by freezing mud in November and eventually exacted 400,000 British casualties. The attempt on the Somme marked the end of any illusions that the war might soon be won. As the British memoirist Edmund Blunden would write years later, many on both sides came to a new realization in 1916: "Neither race had won, nor could win, the War. The War had won and would go on winning."[45] Fussell remarks that "one did not have to be a lunatic or a particularly despondent visionary to conceive quite seriously that the war would literally never end and would become the permanent condition of mankind." At the front, he notes, views were even darker, and it was there that the bulk of what were called the "Neverendians" could be found.[46]

It is this "realization" of the war that marks Frederic's moral development.[47] In the dugout at the front, the peasant Passini tries to persuade a skeptical and still detached-feeling Frederic that "there is nothing as bad as war": "When people realize how bad it is they cannot do anything to stop it because they go crazy. There are some people who never realize" (p. 50). Moments later Passini is killed. Soon thereafter, when the priest visits Frederic in the hospital, he observes: "You do not mind it. You do not see it. . . . Still even wounded you do not see it" (p. 70). "When I was wounded we were talking about it. Passini was talking," Frederic replies (p. 70). Yet by the time Frederic and the priest next discuss the war – after Frederic's summer of convalescence in Milan with Catherine – Frederic has adopted Passini's position. He tells the priest that victory may be worse than defeat because it prolongs the war: "It is in defeat that we become Christian," he says. Perhaps he is thinking of Passini when he says that "the peasant has wisdom, because he is defeated from the start" (pp. 178–9). Frederic himself recognizes that he has changed: "I never think and yet when I begin to talk I say the things I have found out in my mind without thinking" (p. 179).[48]

But Catherine had "realized" the war before the novel began. Her faith in traditional values was blown to bits offstage, along with her fiancé. She already knows what Frederic will learn: that people get blown up while eating cheese; that a good Italian soldier can get shot by Italians for no reason other than starting across

84

an open field; that in the violent and senseless world that this novel portrays, humanity is like a swarm of ants on a log at the mercy of an arbitrary and indifferent fate. She had gone into nursing with the "silly idea" that her fiancé might come to the hospital where she was: "With a sabre cut, I suppose, and a bandage around his head. Or shot through the shoulder. Something picturesque." Instead, "they blew him all to bits." "People can't realize what France is like," she tells Frederic. "If they did, it couldn't all go on" (p. 20). Later, he wants to "drop the war" and get on with the seduction, but Catherine remarks that "there's no place to drop it" (p. 26).[49] Catherine has come to their relationship painfully wiser to the world than is the young man who happens into the war thinking it has nothing to do with him.

She is wiser, too, about the nature of their relationship. In their early encounters, Frederic plots the moves of his "chess game" with Catherine; yet in his callow self-absorption he is oblivious to the fact that she sees straight through his rather unoriginal intentions. She terminates the meaningless banter of their very first conversation, asking, "*Do* we have to go on and talk this way?" (p. 18). And she proceeds immediately to tell him of her fiancé who was killed and of her regret that she naively had "saved" herself for nothing: "I didn't know about anything then," she says (p. 19). The second evening they are together, as Frederic calculates his "advantage," Catherine is smart enough to see the "nurse's-evening-off aspect of it" and find it distasteful. But moments later, as she succumbs to a kiss, she experiences a sudden flash of prescience: "Oh, darling," she said. "You will be good to me, won't you? . . . Because we're going to have a strange life" (p. 27). Three days later, only the third time they have met, she greets Frederic with a rather mysterious remark: "You've been away a long time" (p. 30). Then she initiates a strange dialogue, and Frederic follows her script:

> "Say, 'I've come back to Catherine in the night.' "
> "I've come back to Catherine in the night."
> "Oh, darling, you have come back, haven't you?" (p. 30)

Yet, moments later, after a long kiss, "she came back from wherever she had been" and coldly pronounces: "This is a rotten game we play, isn't it?" Frederic is confused and lamely tries to keep up the game, but Catherine is through for now: "You don't have to pre-tend you love me. That's over for the evening. . . . I had a very fine little show and I'm all right now. You see I'm not mad and I'm not gone off. It's only a little sometimes." When he presses her hand and says "Dear Catherine," she replies: "It sounds very funny now – Catherine. You don't pronounce it very much alike. But you're very nice. You're a very good boy" (p. 31).

Suddenly we begin to understand the drama that must have been playing in her mind both times she had "gone off" and then come "back from wherever she had been": Catherine has cast Frederic in the role of substitute for her boy who was killed and made him speak his lines. Ironically, while Frederic thinks he has been playing a game with Catherine, not knowing or caring what the stakes are, she has been using *him* for purposes of her own, and the stakes are high.[50]

"When people realize how bad it is they cannot do anything to stop it because they go crazy," Passini had told Frederic moments before he was killed (p. 50). Clearly, Catherine has realized how bad it is. "Anybody may crack," she declared the first time she and Frederic talked about the war, and although she was referring to the military lines, the warning applies ominously well to the human psyche. If she is "a little crazy," as Frederic suspects when he first meets her (p. 30), she is crazy like a fox – sharp-eyed about the odds and instinctively calculating the means of survival.[51] Roger Whitlow is quite right when he says that, more than any of Hemingway's other characters, "Catherine has the perception to understand what she must do to restore herself."[52] In the context of the Great War, her willingness – even determination – to sub-merge herself in a private love relationship can be seen as a cou-rageous effort to construct a valid alternative existence in a hostile and chaotic universe.

In his introduction to *Men at War*, Hemingway wrote in 1942 that "learning to suspend your imagination and live completely in the very second of the present minute with no before and no after is the greatest gift a soldier can acquire."[53] In the midst of their idyll in Milan, Frederic reminds Catherine that he will soon have to return to the front, but she replies: "We won't think about that until you go. You see I'm happy, darling, and we have a lovely time. I haven't been happy for a long time and when I met you perhaps I was nearly crazy. Perhaps I was crazy. But now we're happy and we love each other" (p. 116). She herself sees their love as therapeutic, and in her determination to live only in the moment she is, by Hemingway's own definition, a gifted soldier. When she later tells Frederic, "I am a simple girl. No one ever understood it except you" (p. 153), she seems serene and secure in her self-awareness.

Such simplicity has irritated a number of her detractors, whose taste in literary characters runs to the more "fully developed" or who read it merely as Hemingway's inability to create a convincing female. But in her simplicity, Catherine is close kin to other Hemingway protagonists. Nick Adams, for example, another traumatized victim of war, struggles to keep his mind from "starting to work": In "Now I Lay Me," he mentally fishes trout streams, prays for scores of friends and relatives, and methodically replays scenes of his life, backward and forward, avoiding the war; in "Big Two-Hearted River," he concentrates on such immediate sensory images as beans bubbling over a campfire and attends meticulously to the details of trout fishing.[54] Catherine Barkley has been dismissed as a neurotic female by critics who certainly have not then automatically excluded Nick Adams from consideration as a credible or substantive character because of *his* troubles. But Catherine, perhaps even better than Nick, has mastered the tactics of psychological survival.

Certainly, Catherine has developed a keen sense of irony that enables her to maintain some degree of mental control. "One way of dealing with the intolerable suspicion that the war would last forever was to make it tolerable by satire," notes Fussell. Given that the Great War "was more ironic than any before or since," ironic understatement and black humor became appropriate and characteristic means of expression in the literature of the Great War.[55] Frederic's comment about cholera – that "in the end only seven thousand died of it in the army" – is prototypical of this ironic mode, rather than evidence of stunted emotional development or "blunted affect," as has been suggested.[56] Hemingway had employed the tone that Fussell calls "British Phlegm" to powerful effect in the first two sketches of *in our time*, and he uses

87

it also in *A Farewell to Arms* in his characterization of the British major, who declares, "We were all cooked. The thing was not to recognize it" (p. 134). But Catherine's mode of ironic understatement (she *is* British) and her Great War humor most often have been overlooked – her laconic style considered, if at all, as evidence of her underdeveloped character.

It is Catherine who challenges Frederic's statement that nothing ever happens to the brave. When they wonder who said that "the coward dies a thousand deaths, the brave but one," she corrects the statement: "He was probably a coward," she said. "The brave dies perhaps two thousand deaths if he's intelligent. He simply doesn't mention them" (p. 140). They then engage in a repartee on the nature of bravery in a tone of half-mocking self-congratulation, until Catherine cuts it off with a slightly sardonic pronouncement: "We're splendid people" (p. 140). When Frederic tosses off a water glass a third full of cognac, Catherine remarks dryly but sweetly: "That was very big. . . . I know brandy is for heroes. But you shouldn't exaggerate." When he tries to turn the discussion to the future, Catherine's response reflects a "Neverendian" wit:

> "Where will we live after the war?"
> "In an old people's home probably," she said. "For three years I looked forward very childishly to the war ending at Christmas. But now I look forward till when our son will be a lieutenant commander."
> "Maybe he'll be a general."
> "If it's an hundred years' war he'll have time to try both of the services." (pp. 140–1)

Of the British major, Frederic notes that "there was a great contrast between his world pessimism and personal cheeriness" (p. 134). The statement applies equally well to Catherine, and again her humor is a mark of strength and courage in the face of impossible circumstances. After a bad moment of feeling like a whore in the hotel on their last night together in Milan, Catherine transforms the hotel room to "home" by an exercise of sheer will. As she pulls herself together, her stiff-upper-lip determination to put the best face on things is amusing and endearing: "Vice is a wonderful thing," Catherine said. "The people who go in for it seem to have good taste about it. The red plush is really fine. It's just the

88

thing. And the mirrors are very attractive" (p. 153). During their harrowing escape to Switzerland she is able to laugh at how silly Frederic looks clutching the inside-out umbrella he had used as a sail, and, fetching him a drink of water in the bailing pail, she politely replies to his thank-you: "You're ever so welcome. . . . There's much more if you want it" (p. 274). When they finally land, she jokes about encountering the Swiss navy and immediately turns her thoughts to practical matters: "If we're in Switzerland let's have a big breakfast. They have wonderful rolls and butter and jam in Switzerland" (p. 276). Even as she is dying in childbirth, she and Frederic maintain a sense of humor: "I'm a fool about the gas. It's wonderful," she says, and Frederic quips, "We'll get some for the home" (p. 317). In 1920, Philip Gibbs remembered the popularity during the war of a style of humor that he described as "the laughter of mortals at the trick which had been played on them by an ironical fate."[57] His words, written nine years before the publication of *A Farewell to Arms*, uncannily prefigure Catherine's own last words, as she stoically faces up to the "dirty trick" of her own death.[58]

Frederic and Catherine have been criticized for their passivity.[59] But "fighting" in the Great War was a peculiarly passive procedure, as each side, firmly entrenched, simply tried to bleed the other to death. Stanley Cooperman notes that death often came at a moment when soldiers "were either groveling on the earth, fighting desperately among themselves for shelter, or playing interminable games of cards in trenches or rear-echelon posts": "The man was separated from the act; the potential hero could be – and often was – splattered by a stray shell under circumstances that had nothing whatever to do with soldiering."[60] Survival often became a matter not of heroics but of evasion, as Frederic learned at the Tagliamento. Alden Brooks remarked a decade after the war: "Veterans are not men who have learnt how to charge obstacles more furiously than others, but men who have learnt, rather, how to avoid obstacles more furiously than others, and so too, men who have learnt how to disobey orders – or they would not be veterans."[61]

Catherine is a survivor, and, like Brooks's veterans, she has learned to disobey, to avoid obstacles more furiously than others. It is the more conventional Frederic who thinks that they probably ought to get married, and he is surprised to learn that Catherine is not interested: "I thought girls always wanted to be married" (p. 115). But Catherine is well beyond that stage: "We are married privately" (pp. 115–16). "You see, darling," she reminds Frederic, "I had one experience of waiting to be married" (p. 115). After learning she is pregnant, she thinks only "how small obstacles seemed that once were so big" and tells Frederic, "Life isn't hard to manage when you've nothing to lose" (p. 137).

Yet she is hardly a blind romantic retiring from the world at large for reasons of weakness or incompetence. It simply is not her show anymore. Indeed, Catherine's intelligence and resourcefulness and ability to cope in the social world place her in the category of confident and competent characters whom Frederic admires: Miss Gage, who knows how to make a bed with a person still in it, and Dr. Valentini, who is willing to operate on Frederic's knee "tomorrow morning. Not before" (p. 99). Having just lied to the doctor that they had been married four years, Catherine informs Frederic that if they do marry, she will be an American, and any time they are married under American law the child is legitimate. Frederic is impressed:

> "Where did you find that out?"
> "In the New York *World Almanac* in the library."
> "You're a grand girl." (p. 294)

It is Catherine who cannot stand the "legitimate hero" Ettore – "the boy they're running the war for" – while Frederic doesn't "mind him" and still can be impressed that he is going to be a captain. When he asks Catherine, "Wouldn't you like me to have some more exalted rank?" her concerns are pragmatic and concrete: "No, darling. I only want you to have enough rank so that we're admitted to the better restaurants" (pp. 121, 124–5). As Judith Wexler puts it, "he is still playing soldier when she has stopped caring about socially sanctioned roles."[62]

In what Robert Penn Warren calls this "God-abandoned world of modernity," the only meaning and order are what the individual supplies.[63] If Catherine is a romantic, it is in the Emersonian sense. In her self-reliance she is far more advanced than Frederic. She

90

cares nothing for tradition or convention; her values are private and personal. When she checks into the hospital to have the baby, it is clear that her only allegiance is to herself and Frederic, their love, indeed, her only "religion": "She said she had no religion and the woman drew a line in the space after that word. She gave her name as Catherine Henry" (p. 313).

As recorded in the archives of the Imperial War Museum, a Major P. H. Pilditch reported seeing an arrow painted on a notice board marking the beginning of the road to the front line. One end of the arrow was labeled "To the War," the other end "To Heaven."[64] According to Fussell, the Great War — with its "sharp dividing of landscape into known and unknown, safe and hostile," with "its collective isolation, its 'defensiveness,' and its nervous obsession with what the 'other side' is up to" — led to "a mode of gross dichotomy" that came to dominate perception and expression: "Prolonged trench warfare, whether enacted or remembered, fosters paranoid melodrama, which I take to be a primary mode in modern writing."[65] Although she, of course, did not experience trench warfare firsthand, the "paranoid melodrama" of Catherine's world view is not, as some have taken it, evidence of psychological imbalance or female hysteria, but is paradigmatic of Great War thinking: "There's only us two and in the world there's all the rest of them," Catherine warns Frederic. "If anything comes between us we're gone and then they have us" (p. 139). Again, Catherine's knowledge prefigures Frederic's. And again, she is the agent of the "education." Her imminent death is the immediate catalyst for his thematically crucial realization that human destiny is in the hands of an invisible and arbitrary "they," who will kill you in the end: "Now Catherine would die. That was what you did. You died. You did not know what it was about. You never had time to learn. They threw you in and told you the rules and the first time they caught you off base they killed you. . . . Stay around and they would kill you" (p. 327).

Catherine's role in the novel also may be illuminated by another characteristic of Great War literature: frequent references to the pastoral. A pattern of "bucolic interludes" or "pastoral oases" sandwiched between bouts of violence and terror is standard in the Great War memoir, and *A Farewell to Arms* is a model of the pattern in literature. The dynamics of the novel reflect yet another severe dichotomy that Fussell observes operating within much Great War literature: "On the one hand, sanctioned public murder. On the other, unlawful secret love." Such references to the pastoral and to an alternative existence apart from war serve several functions: as "a mode of both fully gauging the calamities of the Great War and imaginatively protecting against them," as well as heightening ironic perception.[66]

Speaking of the British experience on the western front, Fussell notes that what makes the Great War unique and "gives it a special freight of irony is the ridiculous proximity of the trenches to home": "Just seventy miles from 'this stinking world of sticky trickling earth' was the rich plush of London theater seats and the perfume, alcohol, and cigar smoke of the Café Royal." The geography of *A Farewell to Arms* is different, of course, but the Great War theme of the "ironic proximity of violence and disaster to safety, to meaning, and to love"[67] informs the very structure of the novel. The first three books end in short train rides between the hellish front and the "home" of Milan and Catherine, and in Book Four only a few miles across a lake – traversable with difficulty in a night's row – separate a world at war from the peace of Switzerland.

In much of modern literature, as Fussell points out, the Great War become great in another sense: "all-encompassing, all-pervading, both internal and external at once, the essential condition of consciousness in the twentieth century."[68] After Frederic's survival of a fatal shelling, his harrowing escape from execution during the retreat at Caporetto, and their perilous night row across Lago Maggiore in a storm, that Catherine should die in the perfectly natural process of childbirth, attended by doctors in a modern hospital like the place in Milan they called "home," in a place of *safety* – a neutral oasis in the midst of a war-ravaged Continent – is the ultimate irony on which the entire meaning of the novel depends. In his introduction to the 1948 illustrated edition of *A Farewell to Arms*, Hemingway wrote: "The fact that the book was a tragic one did not make me unhappy since I believed that life was a tragedy and could only have one end." If what Hemingway means to show is that war is a permanent condition of twentieth-century existence and that human existence is itself a war with the gods "that can only have one end," then Catherine *must* die. To read her death merely as a consequence of Hemingway's hostility toward women, or his existential fear of complication, or his fictional revenge on his first love Agnes von Kurowsky, or the end that a troublesome woman deserves, is to ignore the whole point of the novel.

What Catherine has taught Frederic about the nature of the world and how to live in it is deeply embedded in his mature retrospective narration of their life together. "It has only happened to me like that once," Frederic reflects. Catherine did bring much courage to this world and was very good and very gentle and very brave. Frederic's thoughts of her are what trigger the famous passage that articulates the central theme of the novel, a passage informed by her own final pronouncement: "They've broken me. . . . They just keep it up till they break you" (p. 323).

> If people bring so much courage to this world the world has to kill them to break them, so of course it kills them. The world breaks every one and afterward many are strong at the broken places. But those that will not break it kills. It kills the very good and the very gentle and the very brave impartially. If you are none of these you can be sure it will kill you too but there will be no special hurry. (p. 249)

In assessing Catherine's character, then, it is critical to remember that *A Farewell to Arms* takes place in a world in which the winner takes nothing, and those who play by the rules only lose more and faster than others. World War I was "a war which had in effect deserted men, which had 'defaulted' from every human value – including the military value of personal test." Stanley Cooperman argues that while "no World War II writer could be serious in making a 'separate peace' . . . or in staking all on a love affair," in the Great War environment, desertion – whether military or psychological – was "the only sane or manly act possible."[69] As Frederic puts it, lying among the guns on the flatcar after his dive into the Tagliamento, "if they shot floorwalkers after a fire in the department store because they spoke with an accent they had always had, then certainly the floorwalkers would not be expected to return when the store opened again for business" (p. 232).

However, Cooperman notes that "the negation of World War I was activist in nature; it was a corrective negation accompanied by tremendous energy in the assertion of alternate values." The typical antihero of World War I literature undergoes "impact," then "alienation," and finally creates "alternatives beyond withdrawal." In so doing, he becomes a hero of the negative act. Within the Great War context, then, the love affair that Catherine offers as an alternative existence can hardly be dismissed or denigrated as trivial, neurotic, destructive, or irresponsible. She is the classic antihero, by Cooperman's definition, who offers "some alternative to the broken world."[70]

Yet in what is all too typical a pattern of Hemingway criticism, even as Cooperman describes Catherine's heroic (or antiheroic) conduct precisely, he never remotely considers her in that role. In fact, Cooperman's reading of the novel is rather anatomically bound. Individual initiative is defined as "virility," or, more specifically, as having *cojones*, which effectively erases Catherine or any other woman from the picture. Indeed, he calls Catherine a "lettuce woman" with no flavor and little flesh. He dubs Frederic the antihero, whose "act of negation" is to regain his initiative "through an exercise of will upon female passivity."[71]

Critical Biases and Cultural Contexts: A Return to the Grandfathers

It is startling to any reader who sees Catherine as the model of self-awareness, stoicism, and courage in the novel that her exemplary strength of character has so consistently and so long been ignored.

One obvious reason is the persistent dogma in Hemingway criticism for the past half-century that Hemingway created only two types of women. With Catherine neatly accounted for as the docile idealized heroine, there may have seemed little else to do with her. Complicating the issue is that the values that Catherine offers as an alternative to the bloody circus of war and modern existence – personal love and fulfillment within the private rather than the public sphere – intersect with our most stereotypical notions about what are merely female concerns.[72] The priest seems wise when he tells Frederic that "when you love you wish to do things for.

You wish to sacrifice for. You wish to serve" (p. 72). Count Greffi can assure him that love "is a religious feeling" (p. 263) and remain dignified, if not noble. But when Catherine tells Frederic, "You're my religion. You're all I've got" (p. 116), many readers dismiss her as a doormat.

Perhaps even more significant than the issue of gender bias in the readings of Hemingway's women is the larger issue of gender bias in literary criticism in general, a bias so pervasive as to be nearly invisible. Nina Baym, discussing nineteenth-century women's fiction, makes the point that "women's experience seems to be outside the interest and sympathies of the male critics whose judgments have largely determined the canon of classic American literature." Baym writes:

> I cannot avoid the belief that "purely" literary criteria, as they have been employed to identify the best American works, have inevitably had a bias in favor of things male — in favor, say, of whaling ships rather than the sewing circle as a symbol of the human community; in favor of satires on domineering mothers, shrewish wives, or betraying mistresses rather than tyrannical fathers, abusive husbands, or philandering suitors; displaying an exquisite compassion for the crises of the adolescent male, but altogether impatient with the parallel crises of the female.[73]

In the case of *A Farewell to Arms*, a number of critics have expressed open scorn for the very values that Catherine represents. They see a concern for personal love as a female weakness, unworthy of serious consideration as an organizing principle of one's life, rather than as a *human* strength. Roger Whitlow, in his vindicating study of Hemingway's women, *Cassandra's Daughters*, clarifies the issue and challenges this assumption directly. He sees that "many of Hemingway's heroes, certainly including Frederic Henry, have two courses of action available to them: the first, the pursuit of a mission that each has convinced himself is of value, usually even worth his own life; the second, the pursuit of those qualities usually embodied in the heroine with whom the hero is associated, the qualities of love, serving, devotion, and domesticity." Whitlow celebrates Frederic's choice of love over the war "mission," which he calls "the product of imagination stunted at the adolescent stage."[74]

Another problem in the readings of Catherine Barkley is that she so seldom has been considered in the context of the novel's specific historical milieu – unlike Brett Ashley, for example, who is nearly always considered in relation to the "lost generation" of the 1920s. While I heartily disagree with his reading of Catherine as "lettuce woman," Stanley Cooperman is absolutely right when he points out that critics whose sensibilities have been shaped by World War II "have often attacked the 'negation' of World War I fiction from their own historical perspective, judging according to political and military necessities which simply did not exist in the previous conflict." He cautions:

> In a period of technological, political, and military chaos, students of war literature have indeed found that there is no "still point in the turning world"; that the heresies of one generation become jejune irresponsibilities of another; that the various aesthetic dictums perfected by one generation are ridiculed by another . . . that the sacrifices and moral gestures of one generation become the cowardice, even treachery of another.[75]

A World War II perspective – in which public concerns are assumed to rightly supersede the private and personal – has influenced our perception of Hemingway's World War I novel and its heroine for decades. Theodore Bardacke, in 1950, criticized Catherine's love for being "a thing apart from the war" and pronounced that "when Lieutenant Henry turned his back on society and isolated himself in Catherine's arms, he decided his own tragedy."[76] Leo Gurko also considers the public arena of war more important than the private sphere of love. He faults Catherine for having "nothing to do in the story except be in love with Frederic": "He, however, has exciting experiences outside the orbit of love. He goes off to war from time to time, is wounded, and manages a thrilling escape." Frederic and Catherine "are, of course, lovers in the romantic tradition, giving up the world for the sake of their love," Gurko says, "but this very defiance is what starves it by turning it inward upon themselves and depriving it of fertilizing social roots."[77] (He also dismisses the central thematic passages of the novel as Frederic's "celebrated little outbursts.") Richard Hovey faults Hemingway for providing inadequate moral guidelines for today's world. ("Though admirable, the famous code is not nearly enough for us now.") And, obviously, he disapproves of the fact that Frederic and Catherine "exist exclusively in and for their love":

> They have not only pulled out of the Great War; they are also cut off from their own families and all friends, and during their six months in a snowy fairyland they have practically no contact with any other human being. . . . They have no idea, purpose, plan; they never consider returning to the world to live in it in any role. They are not trying to learn or understand or grow.[78]

Oddly, in such insistence on social responsibility, one hears echoes of Harold Krebs's mother admonishing the young veteran of "Soldier's Home" to adjust his attitude, find a "nice girl" to marry, get a good job like Charley Simmons, "settle down," become "a credit to the community."[79]

In Hemingway studies, as in literary studies in general, it must be remembered that a critical reading of a text may reveal more about the values of the critic than of the author. The impact of the unstated premises and hidden biases of critics on our understanding of *A Farewell to Arms* has not been adequately examined and is a subject for another essay, if not a book. But as an example, consider the conflicting assumptions that underlie these opposing views of the relationship between Frederic Henry and Catherine Barkley.

In a study published in 1965, Robert Lewis disapproves when he sees Frederic, under the influence of his love for Catherine, become increasingly concerned for the "personal": "He runs to the simplicity, isolation, and irresponsibility of an idyllic life with his beloved."[80] Yet more recent views reflect exactly the opposite assumption as to where Frederic's responsibilities lie. Rather than criticizing Frederic for retreating from his responsibilities to society, James Phelan faults him for selfishly retreating from his *personal* responsibilities to Catherine, citing, for example, his "characteristically unthinking decision to leave her and head back to the front" after learning that she is pregnant.[81] In a similar vein, Roger Whitlow, speaking of Hemingway's next war novel, *For Whom the Bell Tolls* (1940), is critical of Robert Jordan for *not* choosing

> the exit of the "separate peace," the turning away from a venture which could only be as destructive as it would be fruitless, away

from bureaucratic stupidity and insensitivity, toward the deeply personal experience of love and commitment which Maria represents – difficult as such a choice may sound to a world with national, racial-ethnic, and socioeconomic territories which, so the mythology of human territoriality goes, must be defended at whatever cost whenever political and military "experts" claim that such action is vital to some group's "interests."[82]

The earliest critics of *A Farewell to Arms,* those who reviewed the book following its publication in 1929, did not, of course, need reminding of its cultural context. In fact, a comment that echoes through the contemporary reviews is how inextricable the book is from the circumstances of the Great War and how clearly Hemingway is, in T. S. Matthews's words, "one of the most representative spokesmen of a lost generation."[83] John Dos Passos, Hemingway's contemporary in war and letters, wondering over the tremendous vogue for books about the war ten years later, also cast Hemingway as a spokesman for his generation. He is relieved at least that if the "boys and girls who were too young to know anything about the last war" read things like *A Farewell to Arms* and *All Quiet on the Western Front,* "they are certainly getting the dope straight and it's hard to see how the militarist could profit much."[84] And Malcolm Cowley, in his October 1929 review of the novel for the *New York Herald-Tribune,* declared that Hemingway had expressed, "better than any other writer, the limited viewpoint of his contemporaries, of the generation which was formed by the war and which is still incompletely demobilized." Moreover, according to Cowley, most of Hemingway's characters "belong to this category of the un-demobilized," and "their standards are the very simple standards of men at war."[85]

Bernard De Voto explained the book's "limited" vision specifically in terms of the Great War: "It is one experience in the years of chaos and unreason, a chart of the path forced on one atom," and in its "hard surfaced sentimentality" it "completely epitomizes one phase of the modern mind."[86] It is interesting, too, that a number of the early critics, for whom World War I was not a distant memory, seemed to view the novel not so much as a war story, but as a story of love in war. The reviewer for *Time,* for example, claimed that "the novel's depiction of war is on a par with its best predecessors. But it is Hemingway's rendering of modern love that gives the story its greatest significance."[87] Percy Hutchinson wrote in the *New York Times Book Review:* "Dramatic as are the pages dealing with the Caporetto debacle, the war, however, is but a background for the real story, and this in spite of the fact that this story is itself an outgrowth of the war." The "real story," he said, "the love of Lieutenant Henry for the nurse Catherine Barkley, . . . could only have come in the war and out of the war."[88]

These early critics had no trouble accepting a retreat into a private love relationship as a valid alternative existence in a chaotic and unreasonable world. Within the Great War context, it is clear that Henry Seidel Canby considered a personal love story to be a serious subject.

> It is absolutely done; and, even cosmically speaking, the flow of great social resolutions down and away from battle in the Alps to disillusion in the plains until all that is left of emotion is canalized into the purely personal business of love – that is a big enough theme for any novel.[89]

Nor did these early critics have any trouble seeing Catherine as the heroine of the novel. Henry Hazlitt remarked that "the girl, Catherine, has a fine courage and a touch of nobility."[90] And T. S. Matthews, comparing the novel to *The Sun Also Rises,* wrote that the characters of *A Farewell to Arms* embody "a very definite faith." It is "not the note of hopelessness we hear so much as the undertone of courage," he said, and he cited Catherine Barkley as "the principal instrument of the change." Catherine is "an ennobled, a purified Brett, who can show us how to live." She is the "apotheosis of bravery in a woman."[91]

Finally, while again taking most seriously the value of romantic love, a 1929 review headlined "Spokesman for a Generation" presaged the fate of Hemingway's novel at the hands of critics to come, who would read it through lenses tinted by their own historical circumstances:

> He has said, as unequivocally as any author ever has, that to live is a good thing, that to love is a good thing, and that whatever price we may have to pay for these things is not too high. To use a now hackneyed term, "A Farewell to Arms" is a yea-saying book; it is

affirmation, not negation. It is even probable that its sentiment may some day be set down as sentimentality. Every generation is sentimental, but it insists upon being sentimental in its own way, in accordance with its own scheme of values, at the same time branding the sentimentality of its forebears as tosh.[92]

It is interesting that the most recent readings of Catherine Barkley — readings sympathetic to her, appreciative of her strength and courage, and approving of her attempt to make a "separate peace" — seem to be most closely aligned with the responses of Hemingway's contemporaries of 1929. Paul Fussell has noted a striking phenomenon in poetry and fiction of the past twenty-five years: an intense interest in the images and myths of the Great War and their transformation into myths and figures expressive of the modern predicament. He postulates that in eschewing World War II, "these writers have derived their myth the way Frye notes most critics derive their principles, not from their predecessors but from their predecessors' predecessors."[93] And, indeed, a review of the history of criticism of *A Farewell to Arms* seems to bear out Northrop Frye's observation of "a general tendency to react most strongly against the mode immediately preceding, and . . . to return to some of the standards of the modal grandfather."[94]

It may be that post-Vietnam Hemingway critics have more in common with their "modal grandfathers" than with their "fathers." (In Hemingway criticism we have no grandmothers.) Like the so-called lost generation, we again have witnessed a young generation sent off in the name of heroic idealism to a pointless war they could not understand or believe in or even win — consequently to experience an enormous disaffection from the older generation and a society they called in the sixties "the Establishment."

Whether or not this speculation is true, the history of the critical views of Catherine Barkley is a case study of the ways in which the personal and cultural values of critics, their unstated premises, and hidden (even unconscious) agenda can color and cloud our perception of a novel. Under the layers of varnish, Catherine Barkley's outline has been blurred, at times nearly obscured. In restoring her portrait, we must consider her character in relation to the overall design of the work. And we would do best to view her not in the sometimes distorting light of our own times, but in the truer light of her own.

NOTES

1. Arthur Waldhorn, *A Reader's Guide to Ernest Hemingway* (New York: Octagon Books, 1975), p. 123; Francis Hackett, "Hemingway: *A Farewell to Arms,*" *Saturday Review of Literature* 32 (6 August 1949): 32; Peter Balbert, "From Hemingway to Lawrence to Mailer: Survival and Sexual Identity in *A Farewell to Arms,*" *Hemingway Review* 3 (Fall 1983): 40; Millicent Bell, "*A Farewell to Arms:* Pseudoautobiography and Personal Metaphor," in *Ernest Hemingway: The Writer in Context,* ed. James Nagel (Madison: University of Wisconsin Press, 1984), 114.

2. The term was coined by Edmund Wilson, "Hemingway: Gauge of Morale," *Atlantic* 164 (July 1939): 36–46, reprinted in *Hemingway: The Man and His Work,* ed. John K. M. McCaffery (Cleveland: World Publishing Co., 1950), pp. 236–57.

3. Michael S. Reynolds, *Hemingway's First War: The Making of "A Farewell to Arms"* (Princeton, N.J.: Princeton University Press, 1976), p. 261.

4. Clifton Fadiman, "A Fine American Novel," *The Nation* 129 (30 October 1929): 497–8, reprinted in *Ernest Hemingway: The Critical Reception,* ed. Robert O. Stephens (New York: Burt Franklin, 1977), p. 83.

5. Percy Hutchinson, "Love and War in the Pages of Mr. Hemingway," *New York Times Book Review,* 29 September 1929, p. 5, reprinted in Stephens, ed., *Critical Reception,* p. 73.

6. I have articulated this view in detail elsewhere. See Sandra Whipple Spanier, "Catherine Barkley and the Hemingway Code: Ritual and Survival in *A Farewell to Arms,*" *Modern Critical Interpretations: "A Farewell to Arms,"* ed. Harold Bloom (New York: Chelsea, 1987), pp. 131–48.

7. Ernest Hemingway, *The Sun Also Rises* (New York: Scribners, 1926), p. 148.

8. Wilson, "Hemingway: Gauge of Morale," pp. 236–57.

9. Theodore Bardacke, "Hemingway's Women," in McCaffery, ed., *Hemingway,* pp. 346, 350.

10. Philip Young, *Ernest Hemingway: A Reconsideration* (University Park: Pennsylvania State University Press, 1966), p. 91.

11. Carlos Baker, "The Mountain and the Plain," in *Hemingway: The Writer as Artist,* 4th ed. (Princeton, N.J.: Princeton University Press, 1972),

chap. 5, pp. 94–116. In Baker's famous symbolic reading, the "Home concept" is associated "with the mountains; with dry-cold weather; with peace and quiet; with love, dignity, health, happiness, and the good life; and with worship or at least the consciousness of God." In contrast, the Not-Home concept is "associated with low-lying plains; with rain and fog; with obscenity, indignity, disease, suffering, nervousness, war and death; and with irreligion" (p. 102).

12. Earl Rovit, *Ernest Hemingway* (Boston: Twayne, 1963), pp. 69, 106; Waldhorn, *A Reader's Guide to Ernest Hemingway*, p. 123; Balbert, "Survival and Sexual Identity in *A Farewell to Arms*," p. 40; George Dekker and Joseph Harris, "Supernaturalism and the Vernacular Style in *A Farewell to Arms*," *Publications of the Modern Language Association (PMLA)* 94 (1979): 312.

13. Scott Donaldson, "Frederic Henry, Selfish Lover," in *By Force of Will: The Life and Art of Ernest Hemingway* (New York: Viking Press, 1977), pp. 151–62.

14. Leo Gurko, *Ernest Hemingway and the Pursuit of Heroism* (New York: Crowell, 1968), p. 87.

15. Richard B. Hovey, *Hemingway: The Inward Terrain* (Seattle: University of Washington Press, 1968), pp. 76, 85, 87.

16. Robert W. Lewis, Jr., *Hemingway on Love* (Austin: University of Texas Press, 1965), pp. 45, 54.

17. J. F. Kobler, "Let's Run Catherine Barkley Up the Flag Pole and See Who Salutes," *CEA Critic* 36 (1974): 4, 5.

18. Wendy Martin, "Seduced and Abandoned in the New World: The Image of Women in American Fiction," in *Women in Sexist Society*, ed. Vivian Gornick and Barbara Moran (New York: Basic Books, 1971), p. 236; Katharine M. Rogers, *The Troublesome Helpmate: A History of Misogyny in Literature* (Seattle: University of Washington Press, 1966), p. 237.

19. Leslie A. Fiedler, *Love and Death in the American Novel*, rev. ed. (New York: Stein & Day, 1975), p. 318.

20. Rogers, *The Troublesome Helpmate*, p. 248.

21. Joyce Carol Oates, "The Hemingway Mystique," in *Woman Writer: Occasions and Opportunities* (New York: Dutton, 1988), p. 303.

22. Judith Fetterley, *The Resisting Reader: A Feminist Approach to American Fiction* (Bloomington: Indiana University Press, 1978), pp. 66, 71.

23. Two recent studies that reevaluate stereotypical views of Hemingway's women are by Roger Whitlow, *Cassandra's Daughters: The Women in Hemingway* (Westport, Conn.: Greenwood Press, 1984), and Charles J. Nolan, Jr., "Hemingway's Women's Movement," *Heming-*

way *Review* 3 (Spring 1984): 14–22, reprinted in *Ernest Hemingway: Six Decades of Criticism,* ed. Linda W. Wagner (East Lansing: Michigan State University Press, 1987), pp. 209–19. Whitlow and Nolan also provide useful overviews of criticism of the women in Hemingway's fiction, including a number of recent unpublished dissertations.

24. Alan Holder, "The Other Hemingway," *Twentieth Century Literature* 9 (1963): 153–7, reprinted in *Ernest Hemingway: Five Decades of Criticism,* ed. Linda W. Wagner (East Lansing: Michigan State University Press, 1974), pp. 103–9.

25. Linda W. Wagner, "'Proud and Friendly and Gently': Women in Hemingway's Early Fiction," *College Literature* 7 (1980): 239–47, reprinted in *Ernest Hemingway: The Papers of a Writer,* ed. Bernard Oldsey (New York: Garland, 1981), p. 63.

26. Ray B. West, Jr., and Robert W. Stallman, "*A Farewell to Arms,*" *The Art of Modern Fiction* (New York: Holt, Rinehart & Winston, 1949), pp. 622–33; Jackson J. Benson, *Hemingway: The Writer's Art of Self-Defense* (Minneapolis: University of Minnesota Press, 1969); Robert Merrill, "Tragic Form in *A Farewell to Arms,*" *American Literature* 45 (1974): 571–9.

27. Delbert Wylder, *Hemingway's Heroes* (Albuquerque: University of New Mexico Press, 1969), pp. 87–8; Reynolds, *Hemingway's First War,* pp. 254–5.

28. Judith Wexler, "E.R.A. for Hemingway: A Feminist Defense of *A Farewell to Arms,*" *Georgia Review* 35 (1981): 111–23.

29. James Phelan discusses the issue at length in "Evaluation and Resistance: The Case of Catherine Barkley," in *Reading People, Reading Plots: Character, Progression, and the Interpretation of Narrative* (University of Chicago Press, 1989), chap. 6., pp. 165–88.

30. Baker writes that Catherine's death "exactly completes the symbolic structure, the edifice of tragedy so carefully erected": *Hemingway: The Writer as Artist,* p. 116. For discussions of the tragic design of the novel, see E. M. Halliday, "Hemingway's Ambiguity: Symbolism and Irony," *American Literature* 28 (March 1956): 1–22; Robert Merrill, "Tragic Form in *A Farewell to Arms,*" *American Literature* 45 (1974): 571–9; Wirt Williams, *The Tragic Art of Ernest Hemingway* (Baton Rouge: Louisiana State University Press, 1981), pp. 65–88.

31. Wilson, "Hemingway: Gauge of Morale," p. 255.

32. C. G. Jung, *Memories, Dreams, Reflections,* ed. Aniela Jaffe, trans. Richard and Clara Winston (New York: Pantheon Books, 1963), p. 203, quoted in Paul Fussell, *The Great War and Modern Memory* (Oxford University Press, 1975), p. 113.

33. Malcolm Cowley, "Review of *Death in the Afternoon*," *New Republic* 73 (30 November 1932): 76–7, reprinted in *Hemingway: The Critical Heritage*, ed. Jeffrey Meyers (London: Routledge & Kegan Paul, 1982), p. 166.

34. Mark Spilka, "Hemingway and Fauntleroy: An Androgynous Pursuit," in *American Novelists Revisited: Essays in Feminist Criticism*, ed. Fritz Fleischmann (Boston: G. K. Hall, 1982), pp. 352–3.

35. See Reynolds, *Hemingway's First War*, pp. 136–60, and Michael Reynolds, *Hemingway's Reading 1910–1940: An Inventory* (Princeton, N.J.: Princeton University Press, 1981).

36. Gertrude Stein, *The Autobiography of Alice B. Toklas* (New York: Random House, 1933), p. 216.

37. My debt to Fussell for materials regarding the impact of the Great War on the literary imagination will be apparent throughout this essay: Paul Fussell, *The Great War and Modern Memory* (Oxford University Press, 1975). Other discussions of the impact of World War I on twentieth-century literature and on Hemingway's fiction include Joseph Warren Beach, *American Fiction 1920–1940* (New York: Macmillan, 1941); Frederick J. Hoffman, *The Twenties: American Writing in the Postwar Decade*, rev. ed. (New York: Free Press, 1962), especially Chapter II, "The War and the Postwar Temper"; John W. Aldridge, *After the Lost Generation: A Critical Study of the Writers of Two Wars* (New York: McGraw-Hill, 1951), especially Chapters I–III; Holger Klein, ed., *The First World War in Fiction: A Collection of Critical Essays* (New York: Macmillan, 1976), pp. 1–9; Jeffrey Walsh, *American War Literature 1914 to Vietnam* (New York: St. Martin's Press, 1982), especially Chapters 2–5.

38. Whitlow, *Cassandra's Daughters*, p. 18.

39. Malcolm Cowley, "Not Yet Demobilized," *New York Herald-Tribune Books* 6 (6 October 1929): 1, 6, reprinted in *Ernest Hemingway: The Critical Reception*, ed. Robert O. Stephens (New York: Burt Franklin, 1977), pp. 74–6.

40. Stanley Cooperman, *World War I and the American Novel* (Baltimore: Johns Hopkins University Press, 1967), pp. 63, 60.

41. Ernest Hemingway, "Introduction," in *Men at War*, ed. Ernest Hemingway (New York: Crown, 1942), pp. 5, 7.

42. Young, *Ernest Hemingway: A Reconsideration*, p. 245.

43. Robert Penn Warren, "Ernest Hemingway," introduction to the 1949 edition of *A Farewell to Arms*, reprinted in *Modern Critical Views: A Farewell to Arms*, ed. Harold Bloom (New York: Chelsea, 1985), p. 36.

44. Malcolm Cowley discusses the impact of World War I on his generation and mentions the Somme in particular in Chapter 1, "The Other War," in *A Second Flowering: Works and Days of the Lost Generation* (New York: Viking Press, 1974), pp. 3–18.

45. Edmund Blunden, *The Mind's Eye* (London: J. Cape, 1934), p. 38, quoted in Fussell, *The Great War and Modern Memory*, p. 13.

46. Fussell, *The Great War and Modern Memory*, pp. 71–2.

47. Michael Reynolds writes in *Hemingway's First War* that Frederic's desertion is "the final conclusion drawn by a war generation who finally understood what their experience had meant" (p. 282). Others who read the book as a novel of education or moral development include Rovit, Benson, Waldhorn, and Balbert, as well as Dewey Ganzel, "*A Farewell to Arms*: The Danger of Imagination," *Sewanee Review* 79 (1971): 576–97, and Robert O. Stephens, "Hemingway and Stendahl: The Matrix of *A Farewell to Arms*," *PMLA* 88 (1973): 271–80. On the other hand, there are those who see no development or movement in the novel. Gerry Brenner, for example, reads the novel as Frederic's testament before suicide in *Concealments in Hemingway's Works* (Columbus: Ohio State University Press, 1983). See also Bell, "Pseudoautobiography," and Edward Engelberg, "Hemingway's 'True Penelope': Flaubert's *L'Education Sentimentale* and *A Farewell to Arms*," *Comparative Literature Studies* 16 (1979): 180–206.

48. Phelan traces Frederic's change in detail in *Reading People, Reading Plots*, pp. 174–6.

49. Wexler discusses this point in "E.R.A. for Hemingway," p. 113.

50. For a discussion of how the unpublished manuscript of the novel corroborates the reading of Catherine as the one in control, see Spanier, "Catherine Barkley and the Hemingway Code," pp. 145–6.

51. Wexler is among the few critics who have seen Catherine's therapeutic role-playing for the mark of strength and self-awareness that it is, commenting that Catherine "devises a kind of therapy for herself by pretending to love Frederic in place of her fiancé" (p. 144). John Stubbs, too, recognizes their role-playing as a means of "imposing order on chaotic life" and sees the gesture as heroic as well as escapist in "Love and Role Playing in *A Farewell to Arms*," in *Fitzgerald/Hemingway Annual 1973*, ed. Matthew Bruccoli and C. E. Frazer Clark, Jr. (Washington, D.C.: Microcard Editions Books, 1973), pp. 271–84.

52. Whitlow, *Cassandra's Daughters*, p. 19.

53. Hemingway, "Introduction," *Men at War*, p. 17.

54. Wexler relates Catherine's behavior specifically to that of "Hemingway's neurasthenic heroes who compulsively perform the tasks of trout fishing and hunting to control violent emotions" ("E.R.A. for Hemingway," p. 114). Whitlow counts Catherine as "part of a series of Hemingway characters who border on insanity," including Nick Adams, but concludes that she is the most perceptive and skillful in restoring herself (*Cassandra's Daughters*, p. 19). Lewis writes that "Catherine is afraid of herself in a manner that suggests Nick Adams' fear of falling asleep after his traumatic wounding," but he does not conclude that this makes Catherine's behavior similar to Nick's (*Hemingway on Love*, p. 48).

55. Fussell, *The Great War and Modern Memory*, p. 8.

56. Bell, "Pseudoautobiography," p. 113.

57. Philip Gibbs, *Now It Can Be Told* (New York: Harper & Brothers, 1920), p. 131, quoted in Fussell, *The Great War and Modern Memory*, p. 8.

58. The scene of Catherine's death is strongly reminiscent, too, of Melville's description in Chapter XLIX of *Moby-Dick* of occasions "when a man takes this whole universe for a vast practical joke, though the wit thereof he but dimly discerns, and more than suspects that the joke is at nobody's expense but his own" and of times when all of life "and death itself, seem to him only sly, good-natured hits, and jolly punches in the side bestowed by the unseen and unaccountable old joker." Michael Oriard notes that Melville was rediscovered at the same time that Hemingway published his first fiction and that Hemingway read *Moby-Dick* and praised it publicly. Oriard discusses Hemingway's fiction, including *A Farewell to Arms*, in the context of "the post-Melvillean theology of the desperate game" and reads Catherine as the "true player" of the novel. See Michael Oriard, *Sporting with the Gods: The Rhetoric of Play and Game in American Culture* (Cambridge University Press, in press).

59. Bell diagnoses the problems of "Hemingway's pitiful pair" as "affective failure" and views their relationship as a regressive process as they drift into "the dreamless sleep of apathy, the extremity of ennui" ("Pseudoautobiography," pp. 115–16). Engelberg sees Frederic as "almost frighteningly the observer, the somnambulist who stalks the story" and, quite wrongly, I believe, considers him to be an "ahistorical" figure ("Hemingway's 'True Penelope,' " pp. 196, 204).

60. Cooperman, *World War I and the American Novel*, p. 63.

61. Alden Brooks, *As I Saw It* (New York: Knopf, 1929), p. 299, quoted in Cooperman, *World War I and the American Novel*, p. 64.

62. Wexler, "E.R.A. for Hemingway," p. 113.

63. Warren, "Ernest Hemingway," p. 40. This view that the individual is responsible for creating whatever meaning and order life may hold is fundamental to the concept of the so-called Hemingway code. Young's discussion of the code in *Ernest Hemingway: A Reconsideration* is classic.
64. Fussell, *The Great War and Modern Memory*, p. 83.
65. Ibid., pp. 76, 79.
66. Ibid., pp. 235–8, 271.
67. Ibid., pp. 64, 69.
68. Ibid., p. 321.
69. Cooperman, *World War I and the American Novel*, pp. 219, 230–1.
70. Ibid., pp. 189–90.
71. Ibid.
72. Phelan puts the problem this way: "In order for Catherine to fulfill her synthetic role as the agent of Frederic's change and her other thematic role as the exemplary respondent to the world, she unavoidably appears as the image of a sexist male's view of an ideal woman," *Reading People, Reading Plots*, p. 181.
73. Nina Baym, *Woman's Fiction: A Guide to Novels by and about Women in America, 1820–1870* (Ithaca, N.Y.: Cornell University Press, 1978), p. 14.
74. Whitlow, *Cassandra's Daughters*, pp. 21–3.
75. Cooperman, *World War I and the American Novel*, pp. 185–6.
76. Bardacke, "Hemingway's Women," p. 350.
77. Gurko, *Ernest Hemingway and the Pursuit of Heroism*, pp. 86, 90.
78. Hovey, *The Inward Terrain*, pp. 86–7, 210.
79. Ernest Hemingway, "Soldier's Home," in *The Short Stories of Ernest Hemingway* (New York: Scribners, 1938), p. 151.
80. Lewis, *Hemingway on Love*, pp. 47–8.
81. Phelan, *Reading People, Reading Plots*, p. 172.
82. Whitlow, *Cassandra's Daughters*, p. 38.
83. T. S. Matthews, "Nothing Ever Happens to the Brave," *New Republic* 60 (9 October 1929): 208–10, reprinted in Meyers, ed., *Critical Heritage*, p. 123.
84. John Dos Passos, "Review of *A Farewell to Arms*," *New Masses* 5 (1 December 1929): 16, reprinted in Meyers, ed., *Critical Heritage*, p. 133.
85. Cowley, "Not Yet Demobilized," in Stephens, ed., *Critical Reception*, p. 74.
86. Bernard De Voto, "A Farewell to Arms," *Bookwise* 1 (November 1929): 5–9, reprinted in Stephens, ed., *Critical Reception*, pp. 85–6.

87. "Man, Woman, War," *Time* 14 (14 October 1929): 80, reprinted in Stephens, ed., *Critical Reception,* p. 81.

88. Hutchinson, "Love and War in the Pages of Mr. Hemingway," in Stephens, ed., *Critical Reception,* pp. 72–3.

89. Henry Seidel Canby, "Story of the Brave," *Saturday Review of Literature* 6 (12 October 1929): 231–2, reprinted in Stephens, ed., *Critical Reception,* p. 80.

90. Henry Hazlitt, "Take Hemingway," *New York Sun,* 28 September 1929, p. 38, reprinted in Stephens, ed., *Critical Reception,* p. 69.

91. Matthews, "Nothing Ever Happens to the Brave," p. 124.

92. Ben Ray Redman, "Spokesman for a Generation," *Spur* 44 (1 December 1929): 77, 186, reprinted in Stephens, ed., *Critical Reception,* p. 97.

93. Fussell, *The Great War and Modern Memory,* pp. 321–2.

94. Northrop Frye, *Anatomy of Criticism* (Princeton, N.J.: Princeton University Press, 1957), p. 62.

5

A Sliding Discourse: The Language of *A Farewell to Arms*

BEN STOLTZFUS

A Farewell to Arms is the story of a young man who narrates certain events. Frederic Henry writes about the war, his love for Catherine Barkley, and her death, in order to sort through the devastating nature of his experience.

Although Frederic is ostensibly telling his own story, the narrative contains two simultaneous voices: Frederic's and Hemingway's. Together, they give us the simultaneity of a sliding discourse – a simultaneity that allows Hemingway to superimpose two time schemes: one corresponding to the events as they first occurred, the other corresponding to hindsight.

Although the novel is written in the first person, on five different occasions Frederic shifts from the first-person pronoun "I" to the second person "you." In these passages he is not addressing another character, as we might expect, nor is he using "you" in the general sense of "one." Is this a narrative lapse on Hemingway's part, or is the opacity deliberate? Furthermore, in addition to the "I/you" shifts, there are at least four passages in which Hemingway uses the pronoun "we" in a context that does little to clarify to whom, besides Frederic, the "we" refers.

These pronominal shifts are embedded in a discursive weave that contributes to the opacity. It is not until Chapter V that the narrator is identified, an American in the Italian army, and not until Chapter XII that his first name is mentioned in Italian: Federico. The narrator's full name, Frederic Henry, does not appear until Chapter XIII. Meanwhile, he has been wounded at the front and is convalescing in a Milan hospital. Why, we wonder, has Hemingway deferred naming his narrator, and why has Frederic repressed his own name? Partly, Hemingway's strategy is to force the reader to ask who is telling the story, but also, as Gerry Brenner points out, Frederic "is unsure of who he is."[1] Even after his identity is established, the pronominal shifts continue to destabilize it. Names imply differences, and indeed there is a difference between the innocent lieutenant of Book One and the *educated* Frederic Henry of Book Five. The narrative does not only defer identity. It multiplies the differences among Hemingway, Frederic, and Frederic's two selves.

On the biographical level, Frederic's narrative can be construed as Hemingway's displaced version of his love for Agnes von Kurowsky, the American nurse with whom he fell in love in the Milan hospital after he was wounded on the Italian front during World War I. According to her, Hemingway left Europe thinking that she would soon join him in the States and that they would be married.[2] Carlos Baker, quoting Marcelline, Hemingway's sister, says that after Hemingway's return home from Italy, his brooding about Agnes reminded her of someone "put in a box with the cover nailed down."[3] When Hemingway finally received Agnes's "Dear Ernest" letter, he "ran a temperature and was obliged to go to bed."[4] Clearly, he felt her loss acutely, and although, unlike Frederic, he did not sit down immediately to write their story, he did, in time, do exactly that. Also, unlike Frederic, Hemingway had had time to assimilate the experience in order to write about it with a detachment that enabled him to structure it not only as the telling of a story but also as the story of telling. *A Farewell to Arms* is a novel about writing. It is not simply Frederic trying to muddle through an experience that has left him devastated; Hemingway's narrative foregrounds the writer as artificer. The rain motif, for example, which many commentators have analyzed, and whose role as an objective correlative adumbrates the tragedy of Catherine's death, is one of many devices that belie innocent storytelling.

Innocent or not, some readers believe that Frederic is selfish, irresponsible, and infantile, whereas others argue that he is caring and even committed to his relationship with Catherine. Some argue that Frederic is running from his obligations, whereas others believe in his deep involvement. Robert W. Lewis, Jr., for example, argues that Frederic escapes to "the simplicity, isolation, and irresponsibility of an idyllic life with his beloved," but that "in the depths of his mind Henry is really glad that Catherine dies."[5] Ray B. West, Jr., also believes that Frederic tries "to escape from the obligations which life imposes."[6] Scott Donaldson emphasizes Frederic's immature attitude, his selfishness in love, and the heresy of Catherine's words when she says "you're my religion."[7] Faith Pullin maintains that Catherine "is crippled by self-hatred and by the sexual nausea that pervades the novel as a whole."[8] West, on the other hand, sees Catherine's love for Frederic as fundamentally moral, as does Jackson J. Benson, who defends the depth of Frederic's and Catherine's commitments to each other and the caring nature of their love.[9]

Robert Penn Warren suggests that these divergent views fit into a larger context. He says that *A Farewell to Arms* is a love story that establishes a connection between secular love and divine love. He defines Frederic as "the sleepless man, the man haunted by nada," the man who evolves from sensory love as appetite and discovery to another kind of love in which one does things for others: "The priest's role is to indicate . . . the true meaning of love, the 'wish to do things for'." After he leaves, Frederic "muses on the high, clean country of the Abruzzi, the priest's home that has already been endowed with the symbolic significance of the religious view of the world."[10] This is the same "home" to which Benson refers. Thus, Benson and Warren argue that the purpose of the novel is to make Frederic and Catherine's secular love equal in value to the priest's divine love. This is the equivalence that emerges from Catherine's statement to Frederic ("You're my religion.") and the priest's statement concerning love, service, and sacrifice. Arguably, Frederic and Catherine in Switzerland establish this oneness of love – a oneness that Michael S. Reynolds describes as "the spirit of the flesh."[11]

Despite these divergent views, there may be a way to reconcile and even transcend the contradictions – contradictions that are based on the belief that Frederic and Catherine are real people. If we think of them as flesh-and-blood characters, in accordance with the canons of classical realism, then we judge them accordingly. Edmund Wilson, among others, laments the fact that Hemingway "has not shown any very solid sense of character or . . . any real interest in it."[12] Indeed, Frederic and Catherine are not real; they are fictions, mere metaphors within Hemingway's discursive web. Because, according to Jacques Lacan,[13] metaphors veil the presence of the unconscious, or, as he calls it, "the discourse of the Other," critics perhaps should not judge these characters' moral failings or virtues, but instead should analyze Hemingway's linguistic and artistic patterns that subsume them.

Whether Frederic and Catherine are or are not shallow characters, and whether they can or cannot love properly, may be less important than the narrative Hemingway structures around them, because his pattern of pronominal shifts, deferral, and metaphorical slippage casts special light on the changes that are taking place within Frederic. The language of love and death, of desire and loss, of the conscious and the unconscious reveals, if we borrow Sigmund Freud's dream terminology, both latent meaning and manifest content.[14] Metaphors, slips, and gaps in the text – the text's manifest level – veil its hidden meaning. Therefore, the metaphorical resonance of the title embedded in the text requires readerly participation if meaning is to be heard. But the shifts, although not hard to detect, are not always easy to explain. Nonetheless, it is this essay's purpose, within a Lacanian and an aesthetic context, to try to make sense of the pronominal shifts, metaphorical slippage, and structural gaps. A Lacanian reading always focuses on discourse, and because in this case the discourse is Hemingway's, any analysis of Frederic and Catherine must necessarily pull aside the veils they cast on the author who weaves them.

Not all commentators approve of such a critical strategy. Indeed, despite the fact that the first full-length Freudian study of Hemingway's works appeared seven years after *Hemingway's First War,* Reynolds believes that the vein of psychoanalytic exegesis has been overworked.[15] He urges a return to the use of old critical tools, and in using them himself, he provides valuable and useful historical and biographical information concerning Hemingway's role at the Italian front in 1918 and his writing of *A Farewell to Arms* in 1928. Reynolds also provides important details to support his contention that Hemingway researched portions of the novel in order to give it geographical, meteorological, historical, and military accuracy.[16] He points out that Hemingway never allowed reality to interfere with his fiction, that whenever art and biography were at odds, Hemingway "would change the remembered experience to fit the needs of his writing."[17]

The point that Reynolds makes, unwittingly, is that the author's need to write fiction is psychological, as evidenced by the fact that Hemingway changed reality to suit his needs. For example, although both Frederic Henry and Hemingway were blown up at the front, Hemingway was wounded while distributing chocolate at a forward listening post along the Piave River, whereas Frederic was eating macaroni and cheese in the trenches. Although Agnes von Kurowsky and Catherine Barkley were both nurses at the Milan hospital, Agnes had short brown hair, whereas Catherine had long blonde hair. Furthermore, Catherine is a composite character of Agnes, the nurse, Hadley Richardson, Hemingway's first wife, and Pauline Pfeiffer, his second. Hemingway spent an idyllic winter in Montreux with Hadley, and he suffered through Pauline's eighteen-hour labor, followed by cesarean delivery of a healthy child. Pauline did not die, as Catherine does, nor did the baby.[18] Hemingway's novel corroborates certain facts and contradicts others. In this connection, Reynolds's book provides essential information for source hunters, and it says a great deal about Hemingway's working methods, but it tells us little about the meaning of *A Farewell to Arms* as a work of art. Although Reynolds advocates a return to the use of old critical tools,[19] the strategies best designed to reveal what is going on beneath the surface of Hemingway's writing are, nonetheless, grounded in linguistics and psychoanalysis.

Reynolds is correct to stress the fact that it is dangerous to read Hemingway's fiction as biography.[20] However, there are two kinds of biography: One kind tracks the places, events, and relationships of a person's external life, whereas the other records the internal passage. In the second kind, art is the autobiography of the mind and the emotions because it traces a psychic voyage. Thus, Lacanian readings of works of fiction, such as *A Farewell to Arms*, do not concern themselves with the accuracy of historical detail but with language, because language contains metaphorical displacements that correspond to the psyche's affective states. Tropes dramatize the artist's inner world – and its meaning – as opposed to the external, visible world through which the artist moves.

113

With reference to *A Farewell to Arms* there are, psychologically speaking, three fundamental questions: What is the meaning of Hemingway's and Frederic's wound, what is the meaning of Hemingway's and Frederic's loss, and what is the meaning of defeat? Some background information will set the stage for our inquiry. Before Hemingway began writing *A Farewell to Arms*, he and Hadley returned to Fossalta, Italy, in search of the spot where he was wounded by the exploding shell in 1918. Although Hemingway was unable to find the exact location, Reynolds sees this return as Hemingway's ritualistic "attempt to make sense out of the trauma of his wounding."[21] The wounding at the front is the first of three key events in the novel. The second one concerns the massive retreat and defeat of the Italian army at Caporetto. This is the setting for Frederic's arrest and desertion. Why, therefore, although Hemingway was wounded on July 8, 1918, did he choose to set the novel during the two-year period between 1915 and 1917? Reynolds believes that Hemingway must have chosen not to use the Italian victory at Vittorio Veneto in 1918 because "he wanted to place Frederic in the midst of a beaten and partially paralyzed army, not a victorious one."[22] For the Italians, "Caporetto stood for the entire war experience, and that experience was defeat."[23] Although Reynolds gives a cogent historical reason, for Lacan, a sense of defeat always accompanies the infant's state of mind after the so-called *mirror phase*. The *father's law* that separates the child from the mother is interiorized as defeat, castration, and death. Whether historical or psychological, defeat is the bedrock of human experience, and loss is the *sine qua non* of the human condition. All men carry within them not only the invisible stigmata of the primal repression but also the gnawing awareness of contingency, death, and finitude. Reynolds, again unwittingly, senses this when he says that "*A Farewell to Arms* is a massive defeat; there could be no sentimental hope left at the end."[24] The end, the third key element in the novel, is, of course, Catherine's death. Her death and the death of the baby dramatize, symbolically, the defeat of the ego after the *father's prohibition*.

It is perhaps not insignificant that in his youth Hemingway was attracted to older women. On July 21, 1918, when he turned nineteen, Agnes was twenty-six. Later, when he married Hadley, she was seven years his senior.[25] An interesting pattern asserts itself in Hemingway's early years, although as he grew older the reverse would be true: He would be attracted to younger women. There is also the parallelism between an older Agnes who nurses him back to health in the Milan hospital and the role of the mother nursing the child. The novel mirrors this relationship. Indeed, when Catherine dies, and only Frederic remains, we have, replayed, the dramatic sense of the primal triad in which Catherine, the mother, is, for all intents and purposes, lost, and the baby (i.e., the self) dies, both events replicating a child's inner sense of loss and death when the Law intervenes. Only Frederic's wounded ego remains, a silent witness, in the rain, to the massive defeat that has occurred.

If death is a metaphor for separation (absence), as *A Farewell to Arms* most emphatically proposes, then the loss of Agnes, or Catherine, or the mother, in Lacanian terms, echoes the hurt of the child's primal loss when the *phallus* (the Law) represses desire and precipitates the child's accession to language. The consequences of this separation, which are also repressed, are that death and desire form the basis for the so-called discourse of the Other — a veiled discourse that accompanies speech and writing. The discourse of the Other is detectable whenever, as the novel's title implies, there is metaphoric or metonymic interplay. Frederic's desertion from the Italian army corresponds to a rejection of the Law (the father) and the paternalistic order for which it stands. This order is violent and irrational, and it will subsequently be equated with death. Indeed, one of the novel's themes is that death, in its symbolic forms, must be resisted, even though, ultimately, Frederic recognizes it as a force over which man has no dominion. In the final analysis, Frederic's and Catherine's behaviors are symptoms of a metaphoric displacement that is necessarily Hemingway's. Whether Frederic or Hemingway, the father's primal prohibition that separates the infant from the mother is interpreted as a form of death — a death that is repressed but that nonetheless is an accompanying and unconscious piece of psychic baggage. Death and desire are the two components of the Law.

The novel begins with Frederic and Catherine in the Red Cross, on a front they have chosen, but which is not of their making. She is there to forget and perhaps to serve, and he for no better reason than that he is in Italy and speaks the language. Frederic, as Jackson Benson points out, acts like a naive tourist visiting the front.[26] As for Catherine, she behaves the way she does because her fiancé has been killed in the war. She is a person already brutalized by forces that will eventually kill her. Frederic, in contrast, in spite of the fact that initially he acts like a fraternity boy bent on seduction, undergoes a gradual change that will put him in the spot Catherine was in when they first met. He, too, will have been brutalized. Although, at the beginning, Catherine may have been a "little crazy,"[27] she does truly fall in love with Frederic, and, eventually, he with her.

Whatever their private motives for being at the front, their presence *appears* useful and morally responsible. Ironically, this altruism goes unrewarded and is even punished by fate, ignorance, and incompetence. In due course Frederic says farewell to the bungling strategists who are directing the war, and he bids farewell to Catherine, who dies in the delivery room in the hands of incompetent doctors. The novel's title reveals that the linguistic detonator for the succession of tragic events is the word "farewell." Indeed, the trauma of loss explains both Catherine's behavior and Frederic's behavior, because death deprives each of them of the person loved.

At first, Catherine's behavior, because of her "crazy" outbursts, seems puzzling: She slaps him for kissing her, then relents, and in no time is calling him "darling," as though he had become the instant and living substitute for her dead fiancé. Although she is not as calculating as Frederic, she, too, plays the game of love, alternately attracting and repulsing him, even as Frederic fantasizes that she will pretend that he is the boy who was killed in the Somme. Catherine understands Frederic's motives, and she even sees through his artifice, telling him not to lie. She also has insight into her own behavior, and she comments objectively about her first irrational lapses. One evening, having almost forgotten his date with her, Frederic experiences a lonely and hollow feeling because she is ill and not available. Suddenly, her unavailability heightens his love interest. The nature of their sporadic encounters gives her a fugitive and unpredictable role. There are obstacles and a distance, which, Marcel Proust says, are guaranteed to whip a suitor's love into a frenzy.[28] However, it is Frederic's brush with death, more than "the vicissitudes of the heart," that accelerates his nascent love for Catherine. This brush with death mirrors the death of the primal repression. When the Austrian shell explodes,

> there was a flash, as when a blast-furnace door is swung open, and a roar that started white and went red and on and on in a rushing wind. I tried to breathe but my breath would not come and I felt myself rush bodily out of myself and out and out and out and all the time bodily in the wind. I went out swiftly, all of myself, and I knew I was dead and that it had all been a mistake to think you just died. Then I floated, and instead of going on I felt myself slide back. I breathed and I was back. (p. 54)

Frederic has, literally, come back from the dead. His concussion is real and is not without its affective consequences – consequences that are both conscious and unconscious. Whereas the father's prohibition, which is a form of death, deprives the child of the mother, thus frustrating desire, Catherine's appearance in the Milan hospital is like a gift from heaven. When Frederic sees her, everything turns over inside of him: "When I saw her I was in love with her" (p. 91). Why should Frederic's brush with death change the game of love into actual love when his initial goal was to seduce Catherine? How can we explain such an abrupt change? In view of the child motif embedded in the text, a Lacanian reading may provide some answers.

For Lacan, all discourse is always dual because of the repression of desire at the time of the primal scene when the Law, or the name-of-the-father (*le non/nom du père*), cleaves the infant/mother relationship. During this mirror phase, before the separation and irrevocable exile of the self, the mother/infant unit is experienced as a oneness – a longing for the primal oneness that is subsequently incorporated into desire. This sense of exile manifests itself in terms of a paradise lost and as a form of death (castration). The combination of loss and repressed desire (for the mother) coexists throughout life, influencing all behavior and all decisions. This loss is also perceived as an absence. Frederic's need to write his story is a form of repetition triggered by the similarities between his recent experiences and the contents of the primal scene. For Lacan and Freud, the need to repeat is one of the symptoms of the repressed.

Desire for the mother is always repressed because of the incest taboo, but coming back from the dead seems to have resurrected Frederic's desire, and it now focuses on Catherine. She "looked fresh and young and beautiful. I thought I had never seen any one so beautiful" (p. 91). Frederic can give free reign to his desire. The "little stick" of the dead fiancé never was and certainly now is no match for Frederic's convalescing ardor, and so he and Catherine consummate their love – their pretense of a marriage – thus unconsciously perpetuating the illicit and unconscious taboo of desire. In nursing his wounds, Catherine fulfills a maternal role, and although it is a hospital, their nocturnal trysts give the place a semblance of a hotel and the allure of a love that is forbidden. If she is the displaced mother figure, then their lovemaking has unconscious incestuous connotations.

Although hospitals and nurses generally, in their treatment and language (as when using the pronoun "we"), tend to cast patients in the role of the incompetent, or talk to them as children, Frederic's nascent identity, in addition to this hospital syndrome, emerges in a context that is suggestive of childhood. Rinaldi, the doctor at the front, repeatedly calls him "baby." When Frederic asks when the Milan hospital doctor will arrive, Miss Gage, one of the nurses, answers: "Hush. Be a good boy and he'll come" (p. 87). When the doctor finally arrives, he, too, says "be a good boy." The child motif carries over to Catherine, who says "I'm good. I do what you want" (p. 106). These verbal exchanges equate goodness with obedience, and obedience is, generally, what adults expect from a child, or what an officer expects from his enlisted men. However, there is nothing in Frederic's demeanor and behavior, except for his wound and the fact that he is in bed, to suggest that he is a child or that he acts like one. He is young, but he is nonetheless a lieutenant; he answers firmly, he holds his own against overbearing nurses, he pays the porter to bring him cognac, he insists on seeing another doctor when the three incompetent ones advise a six-month delay for the operation on his knee so that the synovial fluid can form, he makes love to Catherine, and he convalesces. Although he is cast in the role of a child, he does not behave like one: He is not obedient, and he opposes the paternalistic order that treats him as an unthinking minor. Nonetheless, death, the concussion, and the child motif reinforce the return of the repressed, the helplessness of childhood, and desire, because desire for the lost mother (the one who nurses) is continuously displaced and renewed.

At some point in Frederic's convalescence, Catherine conceives. Although it is not clear which contraceptives she may have been using (Frederic apparently used none), she says that her pregnancy has occurred in spite of her preventive measures. These protestations are perhaps suspect, but Frederic is too much in love to care or to notice. Although Catherine's conception violates the moral code of the day, they decide not to marry, fearing they will be separated. But this illusion of togetherness is aborted after his wounds have healed, because Frederic is sent back to the front in order to support the paternalistic order from which his wounds had given him a reprieve. His return to his unit is not without irony, however, because the unit has continued to function well in spite of his absence. Moreover, the Law he serves and in whose name the war is being fought almost kills him a second time when he is arrested by the battle police. On the unconscious level, because the ultimate threat is death, these events will be interpreted as the Law's renewed attempt at castration. The sexual implications of linking death and desire point toward Frederic's growing love for Catherine, as well as his determination to endure. Although he endures and survives, he has difficulty adjusting to the events that are gradually overwhelming him.

The passages containing the pronominal shifts reflect Frederic's dilemma and disorientation. I agree with Gerry Brenner, who states that "the novel hangs together best when heard on the heels of Catherine's death."[29] In retrospect, the "we" of the opening paragraph makes special sense if we reread it after finishing the novel. "In the late summer of that year we lived in a house in a village that looked across the river and the plain to the mountains." The similarity in tone and description between this first paragraph with the opening paragraphs of Books Three and Five (particularly the latter) is striking: "That fall the snow came very late. We lived in a brown wooden house in the pine trees on the side of the mountain" (p. 289). Leaving aside the fact that the rain and the snow (the metaphors of fear and death) come from the mountains, it is indisputable that the "we" in the brown wooden house on the side of the mountain are Frederic and Catherine.

Who, then, are the "we" of Book One? The term cannot include Catherine, because she and Frederic have not met. Does it include the other male members of the Red Cross unit? Bernard Oldsey says that the "we" signifies "we the noncombatants, the onlookers not as yet engaged in action,"[30] and that reading makes sense. However, when rereading the novel, and keeping all the pronominal shifts in mind, a more complex view emerges. Could the stylistic similarities in the opening paragraphs of Books One and Five mean that the "we" of Book One refers to an absent Catherine? If so, it reflects an imperious need to write about her and their Swiss idyll when they were as one and lived only for each other. Catherine says: "Oh, darling, I want you so much I want to be you too." To which Frederic answers: "You are. We're the same one" (p. 299). If Frederic begins writing his story immediately after Catherine's death, as I believe he does, then their oneness during the last months of her pregnancy explains his use of "we" in the book's opening paragraph. Frederic needs to understand why she has died and what has happened to him, and in writing the story of their love (she is still too much with him; he cannot dissociate himself from her) Hemingway invites the reader's participation in deciphering Frederic's motives and feelings.

For example, after deserting and after rejoining Catherine at the Grand-Hôtel & des Isles Borromées in Stresa, Frederic says that he feels guilty like a truant schoolboy. Also, "I feel like a criminal. I've deserted from the army" (p. 251). Feelings of guilt surface, attesting a certain vacillation despite his earlier anger that "was washed away in the river along with any obligation . . . it was not my show any more" (p. 232). In civilian clothes he feels like a masquerader. "I had been in uniform a long time and I missed the feeling of being held by *your* clothes" (emphasis added) (p. 243). This use of the possessive pronoun "your" (one of the five passages referred to earlier) alludes to his military self, as opposed to his civilian self. Because Frederic is in dialogue with Henry, the

120

clothes are the outward sign of an inner duality. His name, made up of two first names, Frederic and Henry, connotes this difference. Circumstances (the retreat of the Italian army, his brush with death) force him to desert and to reject the paternalistic order in favor of love, Catherine, and his future child. Frederic is obliged to choose new, radically different responsibilities – confusing responsibilities that are difficult to harmonize with the fraternal order of men with whom he has been fighting.

The degree to which he originally espouses the authoritarian system is illustrated by the fact that he shoots a soldier who would desert the truck that is stuck in the mud. Nonetheless, although Frederic is a man who believes in the system, the paternalistic order treats him like a child, punishing him for making decisions that affirm his manhood. These circumstances and these events explain, in part, Frederic's dilemma, his fragmented self, and his need to tell his story. Catherine's death affirms the dominion of a chaotic authority that is allied with fate. It is "they" who punish Catherine and Frederic for having loved each other. Before dying, she says, echoing an earlier passage, "I'm all broken. They've broken me" (p. 323). And Frederic says "they killed you in the end. . . . Stay around and they would kill you" (p. 327). Within a Puritanical context (Hemingway's family background in Oak Park, Illinois), Catherine's death and their stillborn child can be construed as punishment for an illicit love, because they are not married and have engaged in an elaborate act of pretense in which a hotel room becomes their home and their love affair is called a marriage. Indeed, Frederic and Catherine behave like children playing at love, and when that love is threatened, they blame the world for the afflictions visited on them. Their tragic affair ends in death and separation, and *A Farewell to Arms* is the narrative of the circumstances surrounding the lovers and the feelings engendered by their relationship.

The dialogue between Frederic's civilian and military selves (the "we") refers to a discourse that is trying to sort through the conflicting ideologies of opposing identities. The pronoun "we" carries with it at least three voices (four when we add the Lacanian discourse of the Other): One is realistic, two are imaginary, and one is displaced. The realistic "we" is plausible, chronological, and conventional. It refers to Frederic and his associates at the front. It is the two imaginary "we" voices (Catherine's and Frederic's two selves) that disrupt the narrative conventions of time and plausibility, because they require that the reader keep in mind previous readings of the novel. If the "we" refers to Frederic and the death of Catherine, then her haunting presence dictates Hemingway's narrative strategy. If Frederic writes because he has to reconcile his civilian and military selves, then this additional duality is also incorporated into the "you" passages that follow. This splitting of Frederic's identity fits into a Lacanian analysis.

In writing the story of his love for and loss of Catherine, Frederic is also recovering the wholeness and the unity of the pre-mirror phase – an unconscious phase – but one that nonetheless is now replicated through Catherine's death and the triumph of the Law ("they") – the phallus. *A Farewell to Arms* thus conforms to certain classical phases of Lacanian theory. Frederic truly experiences an ordeal by (Austrian) fire (power) that initiates him into manhood. He is wounded, he falls in love, he recovers, and he returns to the front. Significantly, the shell that almost kills him also deprives him of his pistol (symptom of castration and loss of the phallus). Nonetheless, the "broken baby boy," with Catherine's help, recovers his manhood, even as he convalesces, and before returning to the front he buys a second-hand pistol to replace the one that was lost. The metaphorical value of the pistol is obvious. Its phallic charge is comparable to the little stick – the toy riding crop – that her finacé's mother sent Catherine after he was killed.

"Now we're fully armed," says Frederic (p. 149), in a context in which "I'm fully armed" would have fulfilled the requirements of narrative realism. Why the "we" here? Is it rhetorical? Or is it, as I tend to think, the reflection of a renewed identity and purpose stressing the fact that his civilian and military selves are still one, that they have not yet been sundered, that he still believes in the paternalistic cause that prompted him to enlist in the Red Cross and serve in the Italian army. He does not realize that the enduring enemy is not the Austrians and the Germans but the Law – a Law that is peremptory, ignorant, and incompetent. Frederic's wound, his rite of passage, was a passport to the war-torn country of the Law – the paternalistic system of bourgeois values. Unwittingly,

Frederic begins his farewell in the massive retreat during which "the whole country was moving, as well as the army" (p. 218). This is when Frederic is arrested by the battle police and, in spite of his protestations, is condemned to be shot as a German infiltrator. He has more to fear from the battle police, who are shooting "deserters," than from the Austrians and Germans. His earlier statement that "now we're fully armed" has an ironic echo as he is literally and symbolically disarmed while reaching for his pistol. In the ensuing struggle, the battle police pull his arm up "so that it twisted in the socket" (p. 222).

Frederic says nothing at first about losing his pistol a second time, and the reader has to infer that he does, because there is no other reason for the battle police to pull his arm up and twist it. So it turns out: After pulling himself out of the river, he reveals that "they had taken my pistol at the road" (p. 228). This omission, considering the pistol's phallic connotations, is not insignificant. Frederic's repression of it, in the retelling, corresponds to the repression and loss of memory of the primal scene when the father's prohibition (the Law — in this case the battle police) is perceived as a form of death. Frederic is forced to bid farewell to his arm, that is, his weapon, that is, his military self — his superego. It is this loss that forms part of the "I/you" dialogue. The painful impact of each loss has its psychic reverberations that will be felt metaphorically up to the very end, when Frederic has to bid farewell to Catherine's arms, as he was forced to by the Law when he had to renounce his unconscious, albeit incestuous, desire for his mother.

The title, as every college student knows, and as Oldsey points out, "says good-bye to military arms and to love's embrace."[31] However, *A Farewell to Arms* was not Hemingway's working title, because according to Oldsey he rejected thirty-three projected titles before choosing the one derived from George Peele's poem. The novel incorporates three motifs — war, love, and the education of the protagonist — as overlapping categories within the rejected titles. Contrary to the idealization of love and honor in Peele's "A Farewell to Arms," Oldsey notes that Hemingway's title gives ironic emphasis to the fact that "there is very little glory or honor on the field of battle, and that human love dies in the flesh."[32] Clearly, *A Farewell to Arms* as a title reflects a deliberate and conscious choice on Hemingway's part – a choice that reflects the novel's themes. However, there are unconscious dimensions within the title that reflect the Law (encratic language and the military) and repressed desire (Frederic's displaced love for Catherine).

The pistol scene is a pivotal passage in which the word "arm," as in the title, has two signifieds. The dual reference, to pistol and to a part of the anatomy, illustrates Lacan's theory of the repressed. It is at junctures such as this one – metaphorical junctures – that the unconscious reveals itself through verbal play. Because the unconscious is structured as a language, Lacan insists that we can see it at work, or, at the very least, experience its presence through the play (articulation) of language. Metaphors are symptoms, and in this symptomatic language we (the readers) can decipher the intentions of desire. Frederic is *disarmed* (his pistol and his arm), and he is dealt a symbolic blow that, in time, will also kill the woman he loves. The battle police, whose peremptory attitudes and self-arrogated justice are sources of instant judgment and execution, adumbrate the powers of ignorance that are responsible for Catherine's death (the two doctors at the Lausanne hospital). "The questioners [the battle police] had that beautiful detachment and devotion to stern justice of men dealing in death without being in any danger of it" (pp. 224–5). They speak in clichés, using phrases such as "the sacred soil of the fatherland" and "the fruits of victory" (p. 223). They are the quintessential embodiment of the Law, be it real or symbolic. Firing squads constituted by ignorance are no different than the doctors' death-dealing ministrations of incompetence. Catherine's death forces Frederic to do without the consoling warmth of her embrace. His farewell to arms reinforces the metaphoric significance of the title – a title that contains the two poles articulating the novel's structure: love and death. "It was like saying good-by to a statue" (p. 332). Catherine cannot respond, and a statue does not embrace.

The lesson that Frederic learns is that the world kills: "It kills the very good and the very gentle and the very brave impartially" (p. 249). What he has to sort through, however, are the differences among the battle police, the doctors, biology, and fate, and "they" into which these categories fall, and the world that incorporates all of them. If the world kills indiscriminately, then the absurd consequences of this existential premise are significant. What is also significant is that from infancy on we repress the fact that one of the components of the Law is death — a death whose implications Freud explores in *Beyond the Pleasure Principle.*

In addition to *Beyond the Pleasure Principle,* Freud's treatise on the interpretation of dreams enabled Lacan to show that the operations of the unconscious are themselves linguistic processes. Like the iconic nature of dreams, language and narration have a manifest content and a latent content. In dreams, condensation and displacement disguise the content of the unconscious in the same way that metaphor and metonymy veil the pulsive forces of the author's or the narrator's desire whenever language is being used. If we accept the premise that the unconscious is structured as a language, then all discourse contains repressed material that structures a never-ending dialogue with the Other — a two-tiered identity made up of an Imaginary self and a Symbolic self. The Symbolic is the Law (the father, the army, the battle police). The Imaginary is the displaced self that has to come to terms with the postponement of satisfaction, the repression of desire, the nurturing of discontent — in short, the maturation and acculturation that mark the passage from adolescence to adulthood. Although Frederic's transition from one to the other has been accelerated by the war, he copes competently and even heroically with adversity and change. Still, the pronominal shifts in the narrative reveal cracks in the facade of endurance.

Frederic is always portrayed as bigger than life: He knows his wines, his foods, his women, and his American family, which he rejects. He expounds knowledgeably on guns, birds, fish, brandy, and people. He falls in love. He is not unread. The ninety-four-year-old Count Greffi seeks out his company, and they philosophize about life and death. Frederic is also the confidant and friend of doctors, porters, nurses, enlisted men, hotel clerks, and even strangers. He survives in an icy river, and when he emerges he spends hours in his wet clothes (he wrings them out, but they are still wet) in temperatures that would have knocked an ordinary mortal out with hypothermia. He rows thirty-five miles across a lake from Italy to Switzerland in one night in stormy weather. He endures and he survives — a tribute to his stamina and his re-

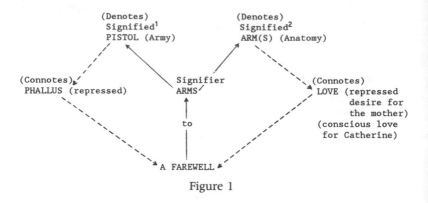

Figure 1

sourcefulness. Perhaps because of the exaggeration, we recognize the attributes of the Hemingway-code hero, and we admire him for his extraordinary attributes. He is one of the initiated.

However, the crack in the facade can be revealed only through language, and it is Frederic's account of his exploits that unveils other selves beneath the one we see. The shifting nouns and metaphors are the gaps and clues that open up the narrative. Metaphors, like condensation in dreams, are paradigmatic. They go from a sign that is present to others that are absent. Reading a trope thus involves a series of operations that occur simultaneously whenever there is an overlapping of meaning. Figure 1 may be useful in detailing the process.

The solid arrows point to the telling of the story, whereas the broken arrows mark the gaps in the story of telling. The signifier ARMS has two signified (S^1 and S^2), each of which connotes a latent and repressed referent. Although the sign (signifier + signified) remains distinct from the repressed referent, the referent, in its contextual and extratextual functions, dramatizes the presence of the repressed. The reader constructs meaning by tracing such metaphorical relationships. Thus, the title, *A Farewell to Arms*, although not a premeditated working title, acts as an unconscious generative cell from which the novel emerges, and like the work itself, the title has both manifest and latent meanings. The manifest meaning is the telling of the story, and the latent meaning corresponds to the story of telling. Frederic needs to tell his story in

126

order to come to terms with loss. Catherine's death is a conscious loss, but it is superimposed on the repressed loss of the primal scene. The novel, in fact, derives its evocative power from this perfect congruence of manifest content and latent meaning, both of which elicit Oedipal feelings in every reader.

In addition to its metaphoric displacement, the word "farewell" has homonyms that slide into the novel's themes. The world treats Frederic and Catherine harshly. In this sense, neither *fares well:* She dies, and he loses the woman he loves. The world, according to Frederic, is not fair, because it breaks the strong and kills the innocent. The world is not *fair,* and neither protagonist *fares* well. They are both trapped, but the trap is as much existential angst, stemming from the certitude of death, as it is the biology of love. Only critics with severe Puritan tendencies could focus on the sexual aspect of the biological trap to the virtual exclusion of its metaphysical resonance.

John Killinger, among others, cogently develops the idea of "the absurd" in Hemingway's works.[33] Philosophers of the absurd, such as Jean-Paul Sartre and Albert Camus, believe that men exist in a contingent world devoid of a priori meaning.[34] The biological trap, in existential terms, posits that all men are mortal and that immortality is an illusion. In Camus's play *Caligula,* the protagonist states it bluntly: "Men die and they are not happy."[35] The death of Caligula's sister, Drusilla, is the beginning of Caligula's madness – a madness that reminds us of Catherine's craziness. Indeed, the death of a person we love (actual or symbolic) cannot be dismissed as readily as many commentators have dismissed Frederic's love for Catherine.

Furthermore, Camus asserts that men strive for immortality in a world that denies such longing. In this context, the absurd is defined as the discrepancy between desire and reality. The notion of the absurd leads to the conclusion that all is not well in a world in which men want happiness only to find that happiness is denied to them. It is not only bunglers, incompetents, and ignorant zealots – the battle police who arrest Frederic and the doctors who perform Catherine's cesarean – who are responsible for premature or accidental death; it is when death is perceived as a biological trap that it affects man's view of the human condition. At such times, life is perceived as tragedy. Frederic and Hemingway can then state iron-ically that the cholera has killed only 7,000. War and cholera are not dissimilar; they both kill. Thus, men are exposed to the vicissitudes of battle, disease, chance, the biological trap, igno-rance, and incompetence. All is not well in this world, and God is not in Hemingway's heaven.

Because the world in *A Farewell to Arms* is sick, the hospital is a metaphor structuring the novel's symmetry. Moreover, as William Wasserstrom puts it, "an affair that begins in a hospital bed in Milan is foredoomed to end in a hospital bed in Lausanne."[36] There is an inversion that takes place from the Red Cross flag to the Swiss flag, which, as Brenner points out, is consistent and appro-priate.[37] The slippage from "farewell" to "well" to "sick" to "hos-pital" to "wound" occurs naturally and consistently. Frederic's wound is tripartite: He is wounded at the front, he is aware of the biological trap as existential angst, and he writes in order to re-cover the object of his loss, whether mother or Catherine. On the unconscious level, Frederic's wound is Hemingway's wound, and both men write in order to recover an absence. The wound–psy-chic-scar idea is also a theme that Philip Young pursues in the "Adventures of Nick Adams."[38] The metaphoric and homonymic slippages and connotations of the words "farewell" and "arms" lift the veil of the unconscious, thereby giving us glimpses of the wound – the primal repression – from which the novel emerges.

The novel's generative cell, the oneness of the mother/ infant unit (Frederic and Catherine's idyll in the Alps), is recaptured pro-visionally in Switzerland. But because Catherine is as much Hem-ingway as Frederic is, they both manifest their author's *desire*. Catherine's quest for oneness with Frederic should not be dis-missed, because her need is a facet of Hemingway's desire, namely, the repressed nostalgia for oneness that is part of every sexual union. A Lacanian analysis suggests that Catherine's death and the death of the baby enable Hemingway to relive the symbolic death of desire. He, the artist, like the child in Freud's "Fort! Da!" game, repeats and relives the game and the masquerade of retrieving the loss of the mother. The artist plays with reality, must in fact play with it, in order to soothe the demands of the unconscious.

128

Although the game metaphor, as Benson points out, is "a meth-od for ethical dramatization,"[39] it also mirrors the absurd and the unconscious. Although not foregrounded in his work as in that of such postmodern writers as John Barth, Robert Coover, and Alain Robbe-Grillet,[40] Hemingway's verbal play is nonetheless present. The freedom to play with language and to invent dramatic roles for his characters emphasizes Hemingway's metaphysical and ethical strategy. Robert W. Lewis, Jr., points out that *A Farewell to Arms* foregrounds many situations of masquerading and playacting. Fre-deric is an American in Italian uniform. He compares love to a game of chess and cards. Catherine pretends Frederic is her dead fiancé. The war itself is ridiculous and a bit theatrical. Patriots, singers, and doctors are not what they appear to be. Frederic hides empty cognac bottles even as he and Catherine conceal their love-making. They go to a fixed horse race. It is rumored that Germans are wearing Italian uniforms. After deserting, Frederic disguises himself first as an enlisted man, then as a civilian. In Switzerland, Frederic and Catherine say they are cousins, and then they say they are married. In the delivery room, Frederic wears a doctor's mask.[41] Life is theater, life imitates art, and not everything is what it appears to be. From a Lacanian point of view, art is a disguise that enables the writer to relive the truth of an experience that never took place but that nonetheless affects the subject with an intensity that is felt to be real. Although Frederic and Catherine are fictitious characters, together they function as Hemingway's meta-phor for loss and desire.

In *Beyond the Pleasure Principle*, Freud concludes, and Lacan agrees with him, that the compulsion to repeat overrides the plea-sure principle because repetition is more primitive, more elemen-tal, and more instinctual. The need to repeat reveals the presence of the death instinct, the drive toward the end, be it the end of life or the end of the story. Freud moves beyond the pleasure principle in order to incorporate death as the essential element of the Other that is repressed. For Lacan, the quintessential paradigm of the need to tell is Sophocles' *Oedipus at Colonus*, where Oedipus says: "It is now that I am nothing, that I am made to be a man."[42] Indeed, he has nothing left to tell but his desire, and it is Oedipus's telling and retelling of his drama that prompts Lacan to say that "it is natural that everything would fall on Oedipus, since Oedipus embodies the central knot of speech."[43] It is Oedipus's tacit recognition and Lacan's conscious exposition of the indissoluble linkage among repression, death, and language that leads to symbolic formulation. "To symbolize," says Shoshana Felman, "is to incorporate death in language, *in order to survive.*"[44] Hemingway's novels are the manifestation of his will to survive, and Frederic's story is the symptom of his will to carry on. If writers write because they have to, in order to survive, then a discourse that dramatizes desire goes to the very heart of language. The author and narrator foreground a fragmented self, projecting it onto the mirror of fiction, where readers recognize the metaphorical image of themselves as the image of the Other.

Why, we may ask, because the use of "you" and "we" as an alternate discourse is such an effective device, did Hemingway not use it more frequently in order to dramatize conflicting sensibilities? Is it because he used it only at critical psychological moments – moments that articulate the text by giving it metaphorical weight? Or do these shifts correspond to some thought process going on within Frederic? There are important passages in which there are no pronominal shifts. There is none when the shell explodes, almost killing Frederic, nor when he is on the verge of being shot by the battle police. Although these passages are central, they are moments of physical action and survival – moments that precede or preclude thought. The pronominal shifts occur only when Frederic is thinking, observing, fantasizing, or remembering. It is thought, coupled with a pronominal shift, that gives special weight to otherwise prosaic passages. Buying the pistol prompts the observation that "now we're fully armed" (p. 149), thus emphasizing it as an important purchase that might otherwise go unnoticed.

The first use of the pronominal "you" occurs when Frederic fantasizes that he is in a Milan hospital with Catherine:

> I would put the key in the door and open it and go in and then take down the telephone and ask them to send a bottle of capri bianca in a silver bucket full of ice and you would hear the ice against the pail coming down the corridor and the boy would knock and I would say leave it outside the door please. Because we would not wear

any clothes because it was so hot and the window open and the swallows flying over the roofs of the houses and when it was dark afterward and you went to the window very small bats hunting over the houses and close down over the trees and we would drink the capri and the door locked and it hot and only a sheet and the whole night and we would both love each other all night in the hot night in Milan. That was how it ought to be. (p. 38)

A straightforward, uncomplicated passage would have had Frederic write "I would hear the ice against the pail," not "you would hear the ice against the pail." The "you" could be construed alternately as an appeal to the reader's auditory involvement, to the generalized "one hears," to his military self (because he is now writing as a civilian), and to Catherine, because he says "we would not wear any clothes." The "you" incorporates all of these possibilities and gives the passage a density that it otherwise would not have. The passage becomes more complex when Hemingway shifts from the conditional tense, "I would," to the past tense: "you went to the window," from which *he* sees the bats hunting over the houses. This is evidence that Frederic is writing after the fact, because the past tense shows that he remembers how it was, when in fact the passage is supposed to be a fantasy of desire. Such ambiguity gives the discourse a simultaneity that combines the past and the present into an ongoing oneness that melds the different voices. The clearest evidence to corroborate the fact that Frederic is remembering while he writes concerns the loss of the Saint Anthony that Catherine had given him. In this passage he refers to the wounding that has not yet taken place: "After I was wounded I never found him. Some one probably got it at one of the dressing stations" (p. 44).

Another pronominal shift occurs in the first three paragraphs of Chapter XXXII. Frederic has escaped from the battle police, emerged from the river, and hopped a train to Milan:

Lying on the floor of the flat-car with the guns beside me under the canvas I was wet, cold and very hungry. . . .

I could remember Catherine but I knew I would get crazy if I thought about her . . . lonesome inside and alone with wet clothing and hard floor for a wife.

You did not love the floor of a flat-car nor guns with canvas jackets and the smell of vaselined metal or a canvas that rain leaked through, although it is very fine under a canvas and pleasant with guns; but you loved some one else whom now you knew was not even to be pretended there; you seeing now very clearly and coldly – not so coldly as clearly and emptily. You saw emptily, lying on your stomach, having been present when one army moved back and another came forward. You had lost your cars and your men as a floorwalker loses the stock of his department in a fire. There was, however, no insurance. You were out of it now. You had no more obligation. If they shot floorwalkers after a fire in the department store because they spoke with an accent they had always had, then certainly the floorwalkers would not be expected to return when the store opened again for business. (pp. 231–2)

Several identities emerge from these pronominal shifts: (1) Frederic, the writer, who remembers the event as he writes about it, thereby conjuring the feelings and thoughts of a past self; (2) a civilian self writing about a military self that has "no more obligations" because floorwalkers who might be shot are not expected to return to the store when the fire is not of their making; (3) a loving self, because his love for Catherine reinforces his civilian identity and its different responsibilities. The sentence "You did not love the floor of a flat-car" (p. 232), combining the "you" and the past tense, argues strongly for a narrative after the fact, for a civilian Frederic somewhere, writing the story of his experiences. It reinforces the hypothesis that the "we" of the opening paragraph of Book One is also these two selves living together in the house in the village "that looked across the river and the plain to the mountains." However, as he watches the men passing on the road, with their cartridges bulging forward under their capes, he says that they "marched as though they were six months gone with child." The comparison, in its incongruity, is grotesque. It can only be prompted by Frederic's remembrance of Catherine's recent pregnancy, thus supporting the hypothesis that the "we," in the beginning, includes Catherine.

Perhaps the most dramatic use of Frederic's "I/you" dialogue occurs at the end, when Catherine is in labor and Frederic is afraid she might die:

this was the price you paid for sleeping together. This was the end of the trap. This was what people got for loving each other. . . . So now they got her in the end. You never got away with anything. Get

132

away hell! It would have been the same if we had been married fifty times. And what if she should die? She won't die. People don't die in childbirth nowadays. That was what all husbands thought. Yes, but what if she should die? . . . She can't, I tell you. Don't be a fool. It's just a bad time. . . . But what if she should die? She won't. She's all right. But what if she should die? She can't die. But what if she should die? Hey, what about that? What if she should die? (pp. 320–1)

This is the dialogue of two antithetical selves: One is responsive to the moral code of the day and feels guilty for not marrying Catherine. The other self considers such a code irrelevant to what is happening and rejects the idea that they are being punished for violating it. One self tries to minimize the gravity of the situation even as the other cannot forget the danger. The fear-of-death self ends the dialogue as the doctor comes into the room. In this passage, Hemingway makes effective use of monologue by splitting it in two, thus heightening the suspense while dramatizing Frederic's dialogic selves.

Having explored these aspects of Frederic's different identities, it is safe to say, I think, that they belong to Hemingway's conscious manipulation of narrative strategy, as opposed to any unconscious symptom they may be revealing. The Lacanian discourse of the Other is not involved in the deliberate pronominal shifts from "I" to "we," or from "I" to "you." There is nonetheless, although displaced, a hint of a mirror phase, mother/infant unit, when Catherine, who has no official religion, says that love is her religion: "There isn't any me. I'm you" (p. 115). Although this is her desire speaking, not Frederic's, as characters they are both extrusions of Hemingway's psyche. Together they manifest his unconscious desire, a desire that, unless transcended, as it is in *The Garden of Eden*, where another Catherine appears, will, because of the nature of the primal wound, always be tragic. As metaphors of the primal unit and of loss and severance, Frederic and Catherine, in their striving for oneness and happiness, unconsciously recreate the bond that is prohibited by the Law, and whose punishment is symbolic death.

The discourse of the self, which is always a discourse of desire, seeks to retrieve the lost object. For Frederic, on the conscious level, it is Catherine, whereas on the unconscious level, for him as for all of us, it is the mother. Our language is our mother tongue, and in using language, as Roland Barthes points out, we unwittingly recover the loss of the mother.[45] Frederic writes his story in order to simultaneously tell us about it, because that is all that he has left. Hemingway has thus given us two simultaneous discourses: the conscious one that Frederic provides and the unconscious one – the discourse of the Other – that accompanies it, which Hemingway's narrative strategies simultaneously veil and unveil.

NOTES

1. Gerry Brenner, *Concealments in Hemingway's Works* (Columbus: Ohio State University Press, 1983), p. 35.
2. Michael S. Reynolds, *Hemingway's First War: The Making of "A Farewell to Arms"* (Princeton, N.J.: Princeton University Press, 1976), p. 207.
3. Carlos Baker, *Ernest Hemingway: A Life Story* (New York: Scribners, 1969), p. 78.
4. Ibid., p. 81.
5. Robert W. Lewis, Jr., *Hemingway on Love* (Austin: University of Texas Press, 1965), pp. 48–9.
6. Ray B. West, Jr., "The Biological Trap," in *Hemingway: A Collection of Critical Essays*, ed. Robert P. Weeks (Englewood Cliffs, N.J.: Prentice-Hall, 1962), pp. 139–51.
7. Scott Donaldson, *By Force of Will: The Life and Art of Ernest Hemingway* (New York: Viking Press, 1977), pp. 155–6.
8. Faith Pullin, "Hemingway and the Secret Language of Hate," in *Ernest Hemingway: New Critical Essays*, ed. A. Robert Lee (Totowa, N.J.: Barnes & Noble, 1983), pp. 172–92.
9. Jackson J. Benson, *Hemingway: The Writer's Art of Self-Defense* (Minneapolis: University of Minnesota Press, 1969), pp. 84–5, 110–11.
10. Robert Penn Warren, "Ernest Hemingway," in *Modern Critical Views: Ernest Hemingway*, ed. Harold Bloom (New York: Chelsea, 1985), pp. 35–62.
11. Reynolds, *Hemingway's First War*, p. 43.
12. Edmund Wilson, "Hemingway: Gauge of Morale," in *Modern Critical Views: Ernest Hemingway*, ed. Harold Bloom (New York: Chelsea, 1985), pp. 17–34.

13. Jacques Lacan, *Ecrits*, 2 vols. (Paris: Seuil, 1966, 1971); Jacques Lacan, *Le séminaire: Livre II. Le moi dans la théorie de Freud et dans la technique de la psychanalyse*, ed. Jacques-Alain Miller (Paris: Seuil, 1978); see also Robert C. Davis, ed., *Lacan and Narration: The Psychoanalytic Difference in Narrative Theory* (Baltimore: Johns Hopkins University Press, 1983); see also *Jacques Lacan: Ecrits – A Selection*, trans. Alan Sheridan (New York: Norton, 1977).

14. Sigmund Freud, *The Standard Edition of the Complete Psychological Works*, Vols. 1–23, trans. James Strachey (London: Hogarth, 1953).

15. Reynolds, *Hemingway's First War*, p. 283. Brenner's *Concealments* was published in 1983. Reynolds's book was published in 1976.

16. Reynolds, *Hemingway's First War*, p. 136.

17. Ibid., p. 170.

18. Ibid.

19. Ibid., p. 283.

20. Ibid., pp. 15–16.

21. Ibid., p. 281.

22. Ibid., p. 104.

23. Ibid., p. 282.

24. Ibid., p. 46.

25. Ibid., p. 175.

26. Benson, *Art of Self-Defense*, p. 82.

27. Ernest Hemingway, *A Farewell to Arms* (New York: Scribners, 1957), p. 300. Subsequent page references to this edition will appear within the text.

28. Marcel Proust, *Du côté de chez Swann. Vol. 1: A la recherche du temps perdu* (Paris: Gallimard, 1954), pp. 188–383. "Swann in Love" is a clinical case description of jealousy and the vicissitudes of love.

29. Brenner, *Concealments*, p. 34.

30. Bernard Oldsey, *Hemingway's Hidden Craft: The Writing of "A Farewell to Arms"* (University Park: Pennsylvania State University Press, 1979), p. 66.

31. Ibid., p. 31.

32. Ibid., p. 34. Reynolds (*Hemingway's First War*, p. 64) prefers one of the rejected working titles, namely, *A Separate Peace*, in lieu of *A Farewell to Arms*, because the homonym of the word "peace," that is, "piece," "would have been a sardonic statement about the love affair." The word "peace," like the word "arms," also connotes war and love, but unlike the caring resonance of "arms," "a piece of ass" has a pejorative meaning that would radically alter the reading of the novel.

33. John Killinger, *Hemingway and the Dead Gods: A Study in Existentialism*

(Lexington: University of Kentucky Press, 1960). In *Hemingway's First War*, Reynolds reproduces pages cut from the published version of *A Farewell to Arms*. These passages clearly reveal the existential dimensions of "the biological trap" (pp. 40–1).

34. Jean-Paul Sartre, *L'existentialisme est un humanisme* (Paris: Nagel, 1952); Albert Camus, *Le mythe de Sisyphe* (Paris: Gallimard, 1942).

35. Albert Camus, *Caligula and Three Other Plays*, trans. Stuart Gilbert (New York: Random House, 1958), p. 112.

36. William Wasserstrom, "*A Farewell to Arms:* Radiance at the Vanishing Point," in *Ernest Hemingway: New Critical Essays*, ed. A. Robert Lee (Totowa, N.J.: Barnes & Noble, 1983), pp. 64–78.

37. Brenner, *Concealments*, p. 28.

38. Philip Young, "Adventures of Nick Adams," in *Hemingway: A Collection of Critical Essays*, ed. Robert P. Weeks (Englewood Cliffs, N.J.: Prentice-Hall, 1962), pp. 95–111.

39. Benson, *Art of Self-Defense*, p. 74.

40. John Barth, *Letters* (New York: Putnam, 1979); Robert Coover, *Spanking the Maid* (New York: Grove Press, 1982); Alain Robbe-Grillet, *La maison de rendez-vous* (Paris: Minuit, 1965). Although James Joyce may be considered a modernist, works such as *Ulysses* and *Finnegans Wake* adumbrate the linguistic play of postmodernist writers.

41. Lewis, *Hemingway on Love*, pp. 41–2.

42. Sophocles, "Oedipus at Colonus," trans. David Grene, *The Complete Greek Tragedies*, vol. 1, ed. David Grene and R. Lattimore (University of Chicago Press, 1954), scene 3.

43. Lacan, *Le séminaire*, p. 269.

44. Shoshana Felman, "Beyond Oedipus: The Specimen Story of Psychoanalysis," in Davis, ed., *Lacan and Narration*, p. 1029.

45. Roland Barthes, *Roland Barthes* (Paris: Seuil, 1975), p. 119.

Notes on Contributors

Scott Donaldson, Louise G. T. Cooley Professor of English at the College of William and Mary, has written biographies of Winfield Townley Scott, Hemingway, Fitzgerald, and Cheever, as well as many essays on American literature and culture.

James Phelan, Professor of English at Ohio State University, is the author of *Reading People, Reading Plots: Character, Progression, and the Interpretation of Narrative* and *Worlds from Words: A Theory of Language in Fiction,* both from the University of Chicago Press, of *Living with Tenure,* and of a number of articles on narrative technique and theory.

Paul Smith, James J. Goodwin Professor of English at Trinity College, Hartford, Connecticut, and founding president of the Hemingway Society, recently completed *A Reader's Guide to the Short Stories of Ernest Hemingway.* In addition to many articles on Hemingway and other writers, he is coauthor (with Robert Foulke) of *An Anatomy of Literature.*

Sandra Whipple Spanier is Associate Professor of English at Oregon State University and the leading authority on the life and work of Kay Boyle. Her books include *Kay Boyle: Artist and Activist* and a collection of Boyle's stories. She has written essays on Hemingway, Hawthorne and D. H. Lawrence, Poe, and Roethke, among others.

Ben Stoltzfus, Professor of French and Comparative Literature at the University of California, Riverside, has published three books of literary criticism on Alain Robbe-Grillet and two on André Gide, including *Gide and Hemingway: Rebels Against God*. He is also the author of three novels, several short stories and poems, and many essays.

Selected Bibliography

Listed here are a but a few of the major contributions to scholarship on Ernest Hemingway. Students may want to consult other volumes as well. Essays in this collection refer to the Scribners paperback edition of *A Farewell to Arms*.

Baker, Carlos. *Hemingway: The Writer as Artist.* Princeton, N.J.: Princeton University Press, 1952.

    ed., *Ernest Hemingway: Critiques of Four Major Novels.* New York: Scribners, 1961.

    Ernest Hemingway: A Life Story. New York: Scribners, 1969.

    ed., *Ernest Hemingway: Selected Letters 1917–1962.* New York: Scribners, 1981.

Baker, Sheridan. *Ernest Hemingway: An Introduction and Interpretation.* New York: Holt, Rinehart & Winston, 1967.

Benson, Jackson. *Hemingway: The Writer's Art of Self-Defense.* Minneapolis: University of Minnesota Press, 1969.

Brenner, Gerry. *Concealments in Hemingway's Works.* Columbus: Ohio State University Press, 1983.

Donaldson, Scott. *By Force of Will: The Life and Art of Ernest Hemingway.* New York: Viking Press, 1977.

Grebstein, Sheldon Norman. *Hemingway's Craft.* Carbondale: Southern Illinois University Press, 1973.

Griffin, Peter. *Along with Youth: Hemingway, The Early Years.* Oxford University Press, 1985.

Hanneman, Audre. *Ernest Hemingway: A Comprehensive Bibliography.* Princeton, N.J.: Princeton University Press, 1969, and Supplement, 1975.

Kert, Bernice. *The Hemingway Women.* New York: Norton, 1983.

Lynn, Kenneth S. *Hemingway.* New York: Simon & Schuster, 1987.

Meyers, Jeffrey, ed. *Hemingway, The Critical Heritage.* London: Routledge & Kegan Paul, 1982.

    Hemingway, A Biography. New York: Harper & Row, 1985.

Nagel, James, ed. *Ernest Hemingway: The Writer in Context.* Madison: University of Wisconsin Press, 1984.

Noble, Donald R., ed. *Hemingway: A Revaluation.* Troy, N.Y.: Whitston, 1983.

Oldsey, Bernard. *Hemingway's Hidden Craft: The Writing of "A Farewell to Arms."* University Park: Pennsylvania State University Press, 1979.

Reynolds, Michael S. *Hemingway's First War: The Making of "A Farewell to Arms."* Princeton, N.J.: Princeton University Press, 1976.

   The Young Hemingway. Oxford: Blackwell Publisher, 1986.

   Hemingway: The Paris Years. Oxford: Blackwell Publisher, 1989.

Rovit, Earl. *Ernest Hemingway.* Boston: Twayne, 1963.

Stephens, Robert O., ed. *Ernest Hemingway: The Critical Reception.* New York: Burt Franklin, 1977.

Wagner, Linda W. *Ernest Hemingway: A Reference Guide.* Boston: G. K. Hall, 1977.

   ed., *Ernest Hemingway: Six Decades of Criticism.* East Lansing: Michigan State University Press, 1987.

Waldhorn, Arthur. *A Reader's Guide to Ernest Hemingway.* New York: Farrar, Straus & Giroux, 1972.

Weeks, Robert P., ed. *Hemingway: A Collection of Critical Essays.* Englewood Cliffs, N.J.: Prentice-Hall, 1962.

Whitlow, Roger. *Cassandra's Daughters: The Women in Hemingway.* Westport, Conn.: Greenwood, 1984.

Young, Philip. *Ernest Hemingway: A Reconsideration.* University Park: Pennsylvania State University Press, 1966.